BUSINESS GROWTH

Also by Niraj Kapur

Everybody Works in Sales (available from Amazon)

The Easy Guide to Sales for Business Owners
(available from Amazon)

How to Sell When Times Are Tough (available from Bookboon)

BUSINESS GROWTH

Lessons learned from divorce, dating and falling in love again

NIRAJ KAPUR

Business Growth

ISBN: 978-1-7391845-0-6

Cover Design: Clare Carroll
Page Layout: Catherine Williams, Chapter One Book Production

Printed in the United Kingdom

Dedicated to my parents
for giving me a second
chance at life

***BUSINESS GROWTH* REVIEWS**

I never read books in one sitting. Niraj's book is different. His personal story is captivating, with hilarious highs and gut-punching lows all over the place. Look out for many important lessons relating the perils of post-marriage life to the best practices of business. It's a fascinating read.

John Espirian, author *Content DNA*

Niraj's vulnerable share of going through divorce, dating, and falling in love again open one up to see how often our experiences and lessons can be applied to more than one area of our life. Sometimes, our most painful moments prove to be our biggest teachers. If you're looking for a book to know you're not alone in dealing with challenges and want to also learn business lessons along the way, this is an excellent read!

Katie Thomas, owner Leaders Online

Your story, the details and heaps of truth have moved me, and will move millions of others. Brave, raw, hilarious, relevant and full of poignant revelations from both a personal and professional level. I loved every second

Loren Greiff owner, Portfolio Rocket

This is a wonderful book by a brilliant man. Niraj shares the many lessons he has learned about business and life. His writing is honest, vulnerable, and wise. This is a book that will both touch you and teach you.

John Spence, America's Top 50 Leaders

Real, raw, and unfiltered. Niraj shares powerful life, business, and sales lessons through his stories of adversity and search for love. He wittily divulges what it's like dating in today's time and his journey of growth. Once I started reading it, I couldn't put it down. This is a must-read book for anyone looking to grow in life and business!

Marcus Chan, Award-Winning Sales Coach and Author of the WSJ Best-Selling Book *Six-Figure Sales Secrets*

In *Business Growth: Lessons learned from divorce, dating and falling in love again*, Niraj shares his journey filled with twists and turns, as well as tragedy and triumph, sharing his raw and touching experiences. I enjoyed how he's able to tie-in and relate a relevant business lesson to each of his experiences. It was amazing, gaining deeper insights and understanding into Niraj's journey through marriage, divorce, the tumultuous world of dating and how he relates to each experience in drawing a business parallel. I strongly recommend this book.

Larry Long Jr, director LLJR Enterprises

Wow – I absolutely loved your book. It made me laugh many times. I also cried a couple of times too. You fully engaged my emotions with your honesty and humour. Some of your phrases were little gems too e.g. 'I was like an open book with torn pages' is just one that springs to mind. Some of your experiences gobsmacked me, nearly all opened my eyes to a world and a perspective I know little about. One thing I can say for sure… this would make a fantastic film.

Louise Ansell, leadership and wellbeing Sky Bounders

CONTENTS

INTRODUCTION

When I got divorced, I never thought my life could get any worse. Then lockdown happened and I was all alone.

I never thought my life could get any worse after my divorce, lockdown and my business collapsing. Then I tried online dating.

Tears. Tantrums. Hysteria. Hormones and lots of drama followed – and that was just me.

During this emotional turmoil and period of uncertainty and confusion, something unusual happened.

My business started to grow.

I didn't incorporate automation, exaggerate my success or use sneaky sales tactics common on social media – none of which I believe in.

I wrote about my experiences.

The fear of being alone aged forty-seven.

The pain of losing so much after twenty-one years of marriage.

My mental health was suffering from going twenty-four hours a day, sometimes several days, without hugging another human being.

Not knowing what the rules of dating were. Getting stood up. Meeting women who looked nothing like their profile. Meeting women who were unhappily married. Meeting a woman who scammed me out of money. The list went on.

The problem I have with women is that I have vintage-champagne taste but a pizza face.

Therapy is unaffordable when your business collapses. So is eating good-quality food, but that's another conversation.

As I wrote about these painful experiences, and related them to the business world, a strange thing happened.

People started following me on social media, specifically LinkedIn, the world's largest business-to-business platform. Microsoft purchased them for $26bn, that's how big a deal they are.

I had a small presence on LinkedIn as a sales coach and I did okay, but I wasn't that successful and I certainly wasn't well known. I came from a generation where you met people and shook hands in business; you didn't make relationships online. We bought from Amazon and Apple of course and looked at our old school friends through rose-tinted glasses on Facebook. This was as far as it went.

People started to engage with my LinkedIn posts. They appreciated my vulnerability and desire to become a better person in a social media world often influenced by artificial success, unrealistic beauty and divisive behaviour.

The majority of my new followers were women, highly unusual in a male-dominated industry like sales. When I asked why they chose me, the answers were, "you are real and honest" and "you are different than other men".

Forget my twenty-five-year sales career in London, multiple

awards, bestselling Amazon books, hundreds of speaking events up and down the UK and fourteen-hour workdays where I missed out on most Netflix shows and pub nights.

People crave authenticity in a world where so many people are trying to be something else.

I reached 6,000 followers, then 7,000, then 10,000 and now I'm on 26,000 followers on a business platform, which now accounts for thirty per cent of my annual revenue.

Recently I was awarded LinkedIn Top Voice in Sales, an award given to only ten people in the world every year. Not the UK, the World. Now, I get asked every day to write about my journey, my life and my business experiences.

That would make it a novel and I'm not a novelist, having written one of the worst fiction novels of all time in 2006, with a female rom-com, *Heaven's Delight*. Ironically, "one of the most badly written novels of all time" was not the worst review the book got. It's currently on sale for £0.08 on Amazon. Please don't buy it. This isn't reverse psychology where I secretly want you to buy it. I've tried to remove it from Amazon and can't.

I was a different person back then, writing for ego and money and not for a desire to help others succeed like I am now.

I want to talk about my dating experiences and relate them to the business world and how they can help you grow. I now run a successful business where I'm lucky to speak in Portugal, Croatia, London, India, Australia, Dubai, Canada and the USA.

I don't just want to give business advice; there's plenty out there. I want to give MY business advice that will help your business grow, through the lessons learned in divorce, dating and finding love again after I'd been kicked to the ground and had to rebuild my life.

There's only one request I have. Please don't read this and move on to the next thing. Nothing happens until you take action. Underline, take notes, highlight, use Post-it notes, even fold the top corner of the page if you're reading on paperback.

You can watch the most inspirational videos and listen to the best podcasts. It doesn't matter.

Nothing happens until you take action.

Names of the innocent, and a few of the guilty, have been changed.

Chapter 1

VISUALISATION

I was happily married for twenty-one years.

Let me rephrase that.

I was married for twenty-one years.

My wife was a force of nature. Women admired her because she was intelligent, resilient, a successful business owner, resembled an Indian Angelina Jolie and always spoke her mind whether you liked it or not.

Men were terrified of her because she was intelligent, resilient, a successful business owner, resembled an Indian Angelina Jolie and always spoke her mind whether you liked it or not.

There's something about my wife and our marriage that shocked people. I'll come to that later.

It all started in the '90s.

It was a funny old decade for dating, particularly being Indian, and you were openly mocked if you joined a dating agency.

If you were English, you met people the old-fashioned way: by getting drunk in a pub, or by getting drunk in a nightclub.

If you were Indian, dating wasn't a big concept. It was seen as a formality for matrimonial purposes and usually through a family friend who knew nothing about you, thus exaggerating your intellect and wealth to any prospective bride's family.

"He has a very big house. A very big car. A very big job." Everything has to be *very big*.

Every Indian family rejected me because I chose to tell the truth. I wasn't a doctor, accountant, pharmacist or first in line to inherit the family business. I lived in a confined terraced house in a bad part of North London and drove a battered Peugeot 205. The only questions Indian parents asked were about money, wealth and savings. Nobody asked if I was a pervert, if I'd ever been a Tory, if I did drugs, if I wore adult nappies or indulged in S & M.

None of these questions were important if you had money.

I would meet a potential bride and our first date consisted of a meeting with her father, mother and often overprotective brother, who sounded like Ali G without the sense of irony or humour.

We'd sit in their living room, which had decorations, expensive vases, gold mirror frames and luxury food served with napkins taken from McDonald's. You were served tea from a posh teapot and given Indian savoury snacks on china plates specifically brought out for the occasion. I have a sweet tooth, so nothing was ever tasty enough.

They would give you several helpings and look at you like you were an alien if you said you were on a diet or not hungry.

It was uncomfortable and you had no power. The woman never revealed her true personality, saying only what her parents wanted her to say and barely saying a word. It was polite, unrealistic and never had a happy ending.

I always swore that when I became a father, my daughter would have a choice. She would marry for love and not money. She would marry whatever man made her happy, regardless of skin colour or religion.

How could you possibly find a suitable match like this?

"Indian marriages are the most successful in the world." According to my father, who never had any scientific proof or government statistics to back him up. "Have one!" he insisted, like I was getting a beer.

"You want me to marry someone I've never met?" I asked. "What if we don't get on with each other and fight over silly things and after a while realise we made a mistake? You know, like an English marriage?"

"INDIANS DON'T GET DIVORCED!" bellowed my father.

He had a point. I didn't know a single Indian man who was divorced. Everyone was married. The men ate while their wives served them. The wives never talked back. The men drove Mercedes and BMWs and the families lived in huge detached homes. Spare rolls of cash were always available in their pockets. Maybe an arranged marriage was the answer. Their lives appeared to be so much better than mine, apart from the baldness, love handles and terrible jumpers.

Still, marrying someone I didn't know? It was too surreal. Despite having Indian parents, brown skin and being tormented by white people while I was growing up, I considered myself westernised. I was so westernised that the Indians referred to me as a coconut; despite my harsh brown exterior, I was totally white on the inside.

I watched Hollywood, not Bollywood. I never went to the temple and sang in church with the school choir and the Cub

Scouts. I preferred the crispy blandness of fish and chips to the spice of curry. I didn't become a doctor like all my Indian friends. They absolutely hated medicine and did it just to please their overbearing parents. Now you know why Indian doctors are so unhappy: they live for a pay cheque, not their patients.

When you have bad luck, it's difficult knowing what to do, especially when you're young. You have no life experience to fall back on.

Business Lesson Learned

I visualised how happy I would be falling in love. How much joy I would have holding the hand of someone I loved. How much comfort I would have waking up with someone I loved. How I would feel knowing my life is better with someone to share it with.

Back then, I had no idea it was called visualisation. Now I have clients create vision boards when they start working with me: that's how important it is, to keep you focused. The bestseller *The Secret*, by Rhonda Byrne, waxes lyrical about the power of visualisation, but it misses the most important part – you have to put in the work. Rumour had it the publishers took that section out. After all, everyone wants quick fixes and most people hate doing hard work.

Visualisation and having a vision board helps you create clarity. It keeps you focused when you've had a bad day at work. It helps you continue when you want to give up. It inspires you when you're tired.

We all need a purpose in life, something that is bigger than ourselves. A strong WHY. This is why vision boards and visualisation, when done properly, create amazing results.

It's your family, your friends, your pets or children. Your dream home. Your ideal holidays. Mix the business with the personal. Have motivational quotes if you prefer. The vision board is not to please somebody else. It's for you.

The visualisation worked and I met a remarkable woman called Rani.

Chapter 2

IT'S NOT WHAT HAPPENS, IT'S HOW YOU REACT

Rani was petite, had the most curious brown eyes and a smile that lit up a room. When we met it was love at first fright. A Halloween house party that my then room-mate was hosting. Don't know why we call them room-mates. We didn't share a room and she wasn't my mate, simply someone who rented a room in the same house as me. Anyway, back to Rani.

Rani was dressed like Catwoman in a mask and a tight leather suit that highlighted her skinny legs and pert bottom. Many people thought she was an uneducated shortarse. I saw beauty, mystery and the forbidden.

She lived in Southall and, unfortunately, spoke like she came from Southall.

"Sick outfit, man. What is you – Dracula?" she asked, holding a plastic cup of red wine.

I wore a black school cape from a fancy-dress shop. The fangs were real since I have pointy side teeth and therefore rarely smiled in public since it freaked people out. As a result, my smile appeared forced or insincere and that wasn't a good look. Luckily, I had a secret sauce: my Northern Irish accent and I played on it.

"It's a pleasure to meet you, Catwoman, so it is."

"Wicked accent. What part of Scotland is you from?"

Only Indians think I sound Scottish or American.

"Did you just call me Scottish?"

"Sorry, I meant Welsh. Fee-fi-fo-fum."

"I'm fairly sure Welsh people don't speak like that, or maybe they do. I've never left Transylvania." I couldn't let her get away with that and playfully approached her, lifting my arms out like a vampire.

She let out a naughty laugh, one the late, great Barbara Windsor would have been proud of. Rani dodged me and weaved in and out of the other party guests, mainly dressed as movie characters.

Jason from *Halloween,* Freddy Krueger from *Nightmare on Elm Street* and Elvira: Mistress of the Dark. You've seen Halloween parties before. These guests were ALL Indians so it looked more surreal. Their continuous hand gestures, vanity and materialistic discussions made for interesting people watching.

I continued to chase Rani playfully. She dodged between everyone, giggling and trying to balance her red wine. Finally, she lost her balance and fell on the bed, managing to salvage most of her wine.

"One minute to get me in bed. You're a pro."

Rani lay on her back. I lay on my side, facing her. It was one of those magical moments in life that you never forget. Eye contact. Laughter. Sexual chemistry. We couldn't stop talking. Our childhoods. Friends. My strict Hindu parents. Her stricter

Sikh upbringing. Living in London. The insane traffic. The mad rush.

After a few hours passed, she became serious: "I want to tell you something cos I really like you and don't want to scare you off."

"Sure." I cared and genuinely wanted to listen.

"This could change everything. You might walk out on me and never come back."

Now I was getting worried. Was it a criminal past? Sikhs don't shave – did she have hairy legs? Was she a member of the Tory party?

"I had an arranged marriage and have three of the most beautiful children."

Rani wanted to reveal more. She held back. I took her soft tiny hands and interlocked my fingers with hers to let her know I wouldn't judge.

"His drinking got out of control and the only way he could cope was by kicking and beating me."

Rani paused, reliving a horrific memory from her past.

"I told my parents and they said if I got divorced, I would shame them and the community. The beatings got worse, so I escaped to a women's refuge with the kids and a suitcase." Her voice became quieter, "And whatever cash I had in my handbag."

I can't imagine how terrifying that must have been for her.

"I worked two jobs, six days a week to provide for my kids. They're my life. I'd like to meet someone who could be a part of that. There's no compromise on my kids, no matter how charming you are."

What do you say to someone who has been through that?

I got up from the bed. Judging by the look on her face, Rani thought I had given up. I took her wine and placed it on the side table. Then I took her hand and lifted her from the bed. We faced each other. "I'm so sorry you had to go through that. I would never ever hit you; I swear."

She believed me. We hugged. Tight. I never wanted to let go and, the best part was, neither did she.

Living in London is incredibly lonely. You can easily go through an entire day without having a decent conversation with anyone. As a man, you can go weeks, months or, in my case, years without even hugging anyone. For me, it was four years in London and Rani was the first person I had embraced.

Four of the longest years of my life. Four years without love. Four years without sex! That would damage anyone's confidence and outlook on life.

It was like a weight had been lifted off me. Hugging Rani made me feel powerful, yet protective of her. This wonderful, amazing, brave woman was what my life was missing.

I wanted our first date to be special and asked if she preferred KFC or McDonald's. I know how to treat a lady, right? We were young and broke and, thankfully, she didn't mind.

KFC it was, with a chicken burger, large fries, corn on the cob and thick chicken gravy which was as flavoursome and moreish then as it is today.

We shared more of our lives over dinner and, the next day, I met her three kids. Upneet, eight, also petite and shy, with long hair. Her name meant "close to heart". Tavleen, six, who looked and acted like an Indian princess. Her name meaning "captivated by God". Manvir, four, innocent with a hint of mischief. His name meant "brave of heart".

Rani was fiercely protective of her kids. Only a few men had met them over the years and none had lasted that long. I realised why. Kids take up so much energy. I'd always wanted to be a dad so I did everything I could to make a good impression.

So naturally our first trip was to Chessington Zoo. We had a blast, visiting the animals and communicating with them like we all spoke English. We ventured to Legoland the weekend after and, after I realised I wasn't a millionaire, we stuck to local parks and leisure centres.

I adored her kids like my own and, over the next year, I would start work in central London at 8 a.m. and finish at 5 p.m., so I could be in Southall for 6.30 p.m. for family dinner. Then homework with Upneet, who was sensible and smart, Tavleen, who was the complete opposite, and Manvir, who was at that age where everything was fun.

Rani and I collapsed on the sofa at 9 p.m. We would whisper how much we meant to each other, then minutes later, fall asleep in each other's arms.

Idyllic.

Now and again, we would wake up in shock when the doorbell rang and her relatives would pop by unexpectedly. Adrenaline would have a field day inside us as we hid photos and all evidence of my existence and I'd rush upstairs and hide. If a relative went to the toilet upstairs, I hid under the bed. Why? Because Indians like to peak in other peoples' houses; that means looking into their cupboards, judging their clothes and especially commenting on jewellery. Due to arthritis, most never knelt to look under the bed.

My parents believed single mothers were damaged goods, an ignorant yet common belief in the Indian community at the time. Not much better now but it's improved. Naturally I didn't tell them about Rani.

Four months later, we moved in together. When her parents would pop by, I would hide upstairs. I couldn't be seen with her in Southall since Indians gossip so much. It made our relationship naughty and lustful; aren't those the best kind? They are, until reality and naivety rear their ugly heads.

"No way in hell are you dating a single mother. Never. Over my dead body," yelled my father.

"Tell me how you really feel, Dad," I replied sarcastically.

"I just did. Are you deaf?"

My parents never understood sarcasm.

"I have never felt this way about a woman before," I insisted.

"Who are you, Tom Jones? Control yourself before I have you neutered." My father was a scary man and a force of nature you didn't mess with. I should have told him where to go, but I was terrified of his bushy eyebrows, the large arm gestures and how he dressed like an Italian mobster with the finest tailored clothes.

"Mum, have you got nothing to say?" I asked, hoping she would stand by her firstborn.

Mum was small in stature. She had a bowl haircut and always smelled of Oil of Ulay. While my father arrived from India by boat with my grandfather in 1951, Mum followed several years later with her parents and lived in Coleraine, a small town north-east of Northern Ireland. The Indian community was small back then, around 300 people, so everybody knew each other.

Mum gave so much love to everyone she met, never judged, never spoke badly. Everybody adored my mother. Despite all these wonderful qualities, she always defended my father. When I was younger, I never understood why.

"Listen to your father and please don't embarrass us again. Promise me you won't break your mother's heart."

There it is. The Indian mother's guilt trip. She had puppy eyes and a sweet, innocent face. How could I say no to that? I'm surprised she didn't mention that she never slept and was always there for me when I was sick.

"When you were a child, I never slept and was always there for you when you were sick. Weekly hospital visits never seemed to end. I put my career on hold. I was there 24/7. Don't make me regret that." And there it was. Unbelievable.

I then spoke to Rani's elderly Sikh parents, thinking there was no way they could be as backward thinking as mine. Rani had forgiven them for not standing by her when she was getting beaten by her husband. I didn't have that maturity and wanted nothing more than to pour ice-cold water over them.

"We'd rather our Sikh daughter was dead than marry a Hindu," was the reply Rani reluctantly translated to me.

I screamed back at them: "Her *Sikh* husband almost killed her! I would never hit a woman! I'm not an alcoholic! I will love her forever and you choose religion over love? What kind of people are you?" I have brown skin so you couldn't tell my face was red, but it was.

I registered the confused looks on their faces. They couldn't speak English and hadn't a clue what I'd said.

Nor did they care. After a year, the only great romance of my life was over.

Business Lesson Learned

In business, you will have bad things happen to you. Many will be out of your control and many will seem unfair. How you react to them defines everything.

Yes, you have to be proactive.

Yes, you have to take action.

Yes, you need initiative.

These are important qualities.

How you deal with problems in life, especially the attitude you have dealing with them, will have a profound impact on your business.

A positive attitude gives positive results. A negative attitude only gives negative results.

The biggest regret of my life is that I let the pressure of my parents and Rani's parents get to me. I should have reacted better.

Chapter 3

DON'T MAKE DECISIONS WHEN YOU'RE ANGRY

I should have fought harder, but I didn't know any better.

For now, I was angry at my parents and her parents for their ignorant behaviour. For putting their narrow-minded and selfish needs before ours.

I had been kicked around, had my time wasted and I was left with nothing.

I stuffed all my belongings into my beat-up Peugeot 205 and moved back into the cold council estate in South Harrow. The posh and privileged lived in magnificent homes only a few miles away and their children attended the famous and unaffordable Harrow school that Winston Churchill had attended.

On my council estate, nobody could hear you scream and if they did, they turned the volume of the TV up to drown you out.

Rani cried. So did I. Over the next few days, we talked on the phone about how unfair this was. One hour a night, then thirty minutes the next night, then fifteen minutes the night after, then a distant five minutes a week later.

Then we stopped speaking. There were no smartphones to

share texts, pictures, FaceTime or WhatsApp. I had a landline and the landline went quiet.

Unable to cope, I put in back-breaking hours at work. Selling magazine advertising on the phone all day till my voice was hoarse. At nights, I would get Chinese takeaways in the office and read competitor magazines. I visited clients all over the UK, travelling long hours by train and getting home at midnight, then working at weekends to prepare for the week ahead.

Months later, I was burnt out. I went to a Soho bar to console myself, not with alcohol, but with chips and mayonnaise. In the '90s, Soho bars weren't that trendy: they had bad lighting, stained carpets, fruit machines and lots of cigarette smoke.

A voluptuous blonde named Pia moved effortlessly up to the bar and ordered a glass of white wine.

Turning away, I muttered, "I've just had my heart broken, I'm not interested."

Why did I say that? Being a nice guy, I turned to her to apologise and she smirked. Confused, I glanced at my reflection in the bar mirror. I had a mayonnaise moustache! I gaped at myself.

"Keep talking, Casanova," she purred, in her alluring Swedish accent.

"Are all women insane?" I asked her.

"That's part of the fun," Pia replied, running her hand through her perfect hair. It fell back into place with ease. Her lips said, "Kiss me," but her eyes said, "I wouldn't dare if I were you."

"Can I get you a drink?" I asked.

Her glass of white wine had already arrived from the barman.

"In that case can you get me a drink? I'm broke," I said.

Pia laughed. "I've never met a man like you." Her eyes lingered on mine for a few seconds, then she took a sip of her wine.

"Wait till you see my man boobs," I replied.

She choked with laughter on her wine. Two hours later, we were back at my place; it was the best sex I'd ever had.

When you're in love, you don't think clearly.

When you're in lust, you think even less clearly.

I missed all the warning signs. After unbelievable, earth-shattering, mind-blowing sex which lasted almost six minutes, she asked me to take her shopping to buy her new clothes and I agreed.

She was married to a man who didn't appreciate her, she told me, showing a lack of loyalty. I forgave her, figuring her husband was a monster and she would leave him for me.

After spending a small fortune on clothes and jewellery every week, she met my work colleagues, who couldn't believe a woman this beautiful was dating me. They were convinced she needed British citizenship, or was escaping prison.

As a make-up artist, Pia was looking for work. I had a friend, Tam, who was making a short film so I introduced them. A few weeks later, as the shoot wrapped up, I paid a visit on set to see how she was getting on.

An elderly woman greeted me with a warm hug that reminded me of my late grandmother. It was Tam's mother. "Pia and Tam are busy if you know what I mean. It's best that you leave."

I was lost for words. Tam's mother flashed her killer smile. "Pia deserves better than you. Cheerio and get home safe." The door was closed ever so politely in my face.

There was no mobile number to call Pia on, because there were no mobile phones, emails or any easy communication method in those days. She would call me from a payphone when she needed anything. I didn't know where she lived and had no way of contacting her.

I walked off the movie set and the crew avoided eye contact. They all knew. Getting cheated on always hurts. Getting cheated on when everybody else knows is devastating and damages your confidence and wellbeing. It messes with any rational thoughts or clear thinking and you're one decision away from making a dangerous life choice.

On the slow train back, where we were all packed together like sardines again, I thought about what an abject failure my life was. Failed career. Lost the love of my life. No respect or relationship with my parents and now I was down to my last few pennies.

I was twenty-five years old and had nothing to show for it.

I was a decent guy! Why was this happening to me? Why couldn't I meet someone and live happily ever after? No matter what I did, I couldn't get it right.

That night I got home, called my parents and agreed to have an arranged marriage.

I've heard stories about the intense heat in India. The humidity is so overwhelming that your clothes stick to your back. There's no air conditioning and all you have are loose ceiling fans which wobble around alarmingly, like they're about to fall on you. In North India in December, however, it was as cold as England!

At least in England, you have central heating and double glazing. In North India, you wear extra jumpers and layer up.

After eight hours on a plane, one hour in customs, then two hours in traffic where everyone communicates by hitting their horns loudly and impatiently, I walked into this rundown bungalow in my T-shirt, shirt, jumper, long overcoat (which was buttoned up), scarf and hat – and I was still shivering.

We travelled to Ghaziabad for my meeting with the future Mrs Kapur. It was two hours' drive from New Delhi. It was densely populated, stray dogs were everywhere and not the cute ones you pet. The road had rickshaws, three-wheeled buggies and smog everywhere.

In a small room in this smoggy industrial town, I met my prospective wife for the first time. We were both nervous.

Priyanka was a diamond in the rough. She had large brown eyes, long dark hair and was a stunning innocent eighteen-year-old. Not quite what I was expecting. At the same time, who knows what to expect from an arranged marriage set-up?

Pia had broken my heart, so I wasn't going to focus on looks. I wanted kindness and authenticity. I was relieved Priyanka wanted to have kids. She had no money, so didn't ask me stupid questions about my salary or how big my house was.

Similarly, I would get no dowry (common in Indian marriages, where the woman's family gives a "financial gift", varying from a new bedroom to a lump sum of money, to a car).

Priyanka also spoke good English since teachers in certain Indian schools teach in English, not Hindi. She was an amazing cook, liked *The Simpsons,* enjoyed Bollywood movies, loved Celine Dion and wanted to get married. So, after twenty minutes, I agreed to marry her.

Talk about a shocker. Twenty minutes to decide on marriage. It often takes me longer to pick a Chinese takeaway.

Four days later our wedding day was packed with 600 people I had never met in my life. I only knew fourteen of them. My parents, sister, aunts and Priyanka's immediate family.

For the first time in almost a decade I saw my parents happy and proud. I don't know why their approval meant so much to me but at that moment it was all that mattered. Despite being overwhelmed by the occasion and the ceremony, which lasted three days and nights, I didn't want to let my parents down. I promised myself I would do everything I could to make the marriage work.

Forty-eight hours later, I wanted a divorce.

Business Lessons Learned

Never make a decision when you're angry or upset. It's usually the wrong decision. Go for a walk, clear your head, think things though and write down your thoughts. Sometimes you can leave things for twenty-four hours before you reply.

Instant reactions don't always work, especially when making huge decisions. When you make a mistake, apologise quickly and sincerely. People will usually understand and accept that. Dragging things out and letting your ego get in the way only makes things worse.

It's okay to make mistakes. It's not okay to make the same mistake twice.

The best advice my first coach ever gave to me was "focus on the problem, not the person".

Chapter 4

MONEY

We arrived back in England. It was becoming extremely apparent that we had nothing in common. It was tough to get past.

Priyanka had left everything behind, flying thousands of miles from New Delhi to London to start life as a married woman. Unfortunately, India was not full of billionaires and millionaires in the '90s like it is now.

Not many people had travelled and there was limited internet, so their experience of the world was through Bollywood movies. Here's what they all thought:

- Everyone in London lived in a mansion.
- Everyone spoke like the Queen.
- Everyone was singing and dancing.
- Everyone had money.
- Everyone had a white servant.
- Everyone drove a Mini or Range Rover.

In reality, this was the council estate I lived on:

- If you attempted conversation, people thought you were weird and avoided you.
- If you smiled, people would look at you with utter confusion.
- Everyone sounded like Ray Winstone.
- Single mums on benefits wore nicer clothes than my wife.
- Children on benefits wore nicer clothes than we did.

There were also little differences in culture. When Indians arrived in England, they usually only mixed with other Indians. That's like being English, going to Spain on holiday and only spending time with English people – what a waste. We're so lucky to have so many different cultures and religions in the UK, yet most of them don't mix.

In India, people don't say "thank you". That drove me mad, because I always say "thank you". So does every English person I know. Priyanka didn't. Neither did her family. They weren't rude. In fact, my in-laws were wonderful, caring people, but not saying thanks did confuse and irk me.

Indians speak their mind whether you like it or not. English people are more polite and often don't say what they mean for fear of offending anyone.

Priyanka was eighteen and a virgin; I was twenty-five. We were both far too young to get married. I never understood or appreciated how tough it must be for someone so young to leave her family and life behind and move to a completely different country halfway across the world.

We had no family nearby, no friends and no money to go

out with. Calling India was expensive back then, so I had to limit our calls to one hour a week, and no matter how nicely you do your house up, a rundown council estate is still a rundown council estate.

I made matters worse by coming home from work at 7 p.m., eating a delicious meal that Priyanka had spent hours preparing and being too tired to speak. She never said a word. We were so different. It was never going to work.

I was too scared to tell my parents it wasn't working. Priyanka didn't want to bring shame to her family, so said nothing either. And on and on we lived in a bubble of our own misery.

When our daughter Freya was born, everything changed. Suddenly, we had a purpose. We both fell in love with this adorable baby girl who looked like me, so everyone thought she was a boy! Being parents made us better people and brought us closer together.

Most men at that time choose a career over a family. I did the opposite. Not because I'm Irish, but because family gave my career more meaning than doing a nine-to-five job for somebody else.

Office work is boring. I'm sorry, but somebody has to say it.

Now, I wanted to make sure my family were comfortable. I worked day and night in my career to achieve success. I got promoted from sales executive to sales manager to global sales manager and I travelled the world on business.

We moved to Milton Keynes in Buckinghamshire, which had beautiful lakes, stunning woods and more lush green trees than anywhere else in the UK.

Priyanka won student of the year at the London College of

Beauty Therapy, where she had to commute to from our home fifty miles away with Freya, dropping her off at my office at 5 p.m. then studying while I took Freya home in rush hour in a buggy.

I discovered that conservative British people (who generally prefer to sweep things under the carpet) tend to express themselves to the extreme in three situations: adding milk to a cup then adding tea, car rage and parents carrying buggies in rush hour.

Priyanka set up a beauty salon by herself, with simple manicures, pedicures and massages. She transformed it into a successful business with laser hair-removal machines, non-surgical facelift treatments and several staff.

Ladies of leisure and successful businesswomen visited every week for treatments and products. She bought her own car and she put two brothers through university, which was admirable. As an immigrant, she achieved more than any of the local therapists who were born and brought up in England did.

Freya was a straight-A student. She was a quiet, shy girl and worked hard. I picked her up from the babysitter every night at 7.30 p.m. when I finished the long, miserable commute home from London. That would give us less than ninety minutes to get home, cook dinner and spend time together. Then at 9 p.m. Priyanka would arrive from the salon, having put in a back-breaking twelve-hour day.

Although we were the parents, Freya often took care of us. She made us tea, gave us head massages, told us she loved us and made us laugh with her curiosity. She always did her own homework and assignments on time.

The fighting started when she became a teenager: having temper tantrums, being ungrateful, shouting, being hormonal – just to be clear that was me, not Freya. It's so difficult seeing your child grow up.

They're embarrassed to be seen with you in public. They don't show you the respect you believe you deserve. They talk back. They test your boundaries. You know that hitting them is wrong, yet all you want to do is hit them.

During this time, Freya became closer to her mum. Freya and I slowly drifted apart. I could handle corporate London, the tension, stress, long hours, massive egos, overseas travel, intense pressure of hitting high targets, but having a teenage daughter was a different level of awfulness.

Tragically, Freya and I would never become that close again.

Priyanka and I excelled in our careers so we upgraded to the perfect country home in Milton Keynes with acres of greenery and a private driveway in a gated land of only six houses.

It had been our dream to own a country house. For me, it was a status symbol to show I had made it and I believed money would make me happy. For Priyanka, it was much deeper. Her father had died of cancer when she was thirteen and their family home was destroyed by corrupt businessmen who had claimed they owned part of it; this is common in India, since there weren't many written business contracts back then. Deals were done on handshakes.

My mother-in-law refused to give in to these crooks and stood her ground as they bulldozed the back of her house. The rubble stood there for years. The only visitors were stray dogs and rats, who often made it into the bungalow.

I can't imagine how unbearable that must have been for a

woman who had just lost her husband and how scary it must have been for Priyanka and her siblings. My mother-in-law really was quite a remarkable person.

Everyone saw Priyanka and I as the perfect couple.

Guests would be wowed by the space and size of our fabulous three-storey home. I couldn't believe how lucky I was. Priyanka and I had a stunning, picturesque English home, expensive cars and an amazing daughter. Life was good. We weren't in love, but there was mutual respect between us. In other words, it was a typical Indian marriage.

So what happens when you make money your master and achieve your financial dreams? It's a long bumpy road full of potholes to the bottom.

Priyanka continued to be consistently brilliant. I got tired of twenty-three years of commuting into London and set up my own business, which caused huge financial heartache. I jumped in head-first, without a clue as to how hard it would be to run a business. I earned peanuts as a coach. I didn't understand pricing or negotiation and, with no big corporate name behind me, I was a nobody.

This naturally put a huge strain on our marriage. Even so, for twelve exceptionally long months, Priyanka kindly supported me.

Our savings were drained. I suffered from the humiliation and fragile male ego of having my wife support me, frustrated that I couldn't make a business work, frustrated that most people don't give a damn about small businesses, and depression reared its ugly head.

Freya went to university and it was just the two of us, again. The home we had built became a house. Suddenly, you could hear the boiler switch on or the neighbour's car pull up. It was the long, cruel sound of silence. I could totally identify with the stress parents endure when their child or children leave home.

Priyanka and I tried date nights, but the conversation was so bland and boring we often ended up saying nothing and spent the night on our phones or watching TV in separate rooms. It's amazing how you can live in the same house as someone and be so apart.

We flew to the mountains of Northern India for her younger brother's spectacular wedding but fought day and night because we both knew the marriage was over. My depression became worse. I lacked focus and couldn't sleep at night.

Resentment kicked in. Priyanka complained that I never listened. I can't remember, I wasn't paying attention.

When we got back to England, I went to see a divorce lawyer for advice. Amy was considerate and took good care of me as her client, the polar opposite of the typical scumbag solicitors we're expected to deal with. Once I'd told Priyanka what I'd done, that I'd simply visited a solicitor for advice and options, she went ballistic and I couldn't reason with her.

Anytime we spoke it was a mix of screaming, blurting profanities or tears, as we both tried to process the pain of losing twenty-one years together.

Two friends, with whom we'd spent Christmas, Diwali, picnics in the summer, gin festivals and children's birthdays, refused to speak to me and took Priyanka's side. That broke my heart. Seven years of friendship gone. They treated me like I didn't exist.

We all want to have our voices heard, to be respected and to know that we matter. I felt like I didn't matter to anybody.

My parents turned against me. They were humiliated by my decision and kept nagging at me to change my mind. They made no effort to understand what I was going through, yet I felt so ashamed for hurting them.

Unfortunately, depression can destroy you in ways you can't imagine. It stops you from seeing clearly. No matter how hard you visualise you can't see beyond a wall of darkness.

I thought my life couldn't get any worse.

Then I wrote my suicide letter.

Business Lesson Learned

Money is alluring. It makes us believe we can achieve happiness. This is one of the world's biggest myths. Money amplifies who you are. If you're unhappy, being rich makes you more unhappy. If you're kind and happy, being rich makes you more generous. It took me a long time to understand that.

With money, you can make society better, support your family, invest in your future, enjoy new experiences. It is wonderful. It's not the most important thing out there.

In business, focus on helping the client first, not on making money first.

Jim Carrey once said, "I wish everyone could be rich and famous and get everything they dreamed of so they can see it's not the answer."

A favourite quote of mine from Barack Obama: "Focusing your life solely on making a buck shows a poverty of ambition. It asks too little of yourself. And it will leave you unfulfilled."

Chapter 5

LEARNING TO PIVOT

There are certain things you never say to a woman during a divorce.

"You're attractive so you will easily get over this."

"Can I borrow some money?"

"What's for dinner tonight?"

I know this because I said these to Priyanka on several occasions.

I should add another one. This is the most important thing never to say to a woman when emotions are high.

"Can you just calm down?"

At least I didn't say, "What's wrong, are you on your period?" Okay, I did, but every man does that at least once. You can imagine where that conversation went.

Twenty-one years of anger, betrayal and frustration poured out of Priyanka. She remembered mistakes I'd made fifteen years ago. The day, the time, even the weather!

The time when she was pregnant, and I told her I didn't want to be a father. I don't recall that.

The time when I told her I had a large car when I actually drove a second-hand Peugeot 205. I don't recall that.

The time when I told her I never think about other women, although in my defence every man tells that lie.

She told my parents how I had emptied our daughter's university savings account to fund my own Hollywood screenwriting dream. Sadly, that is true and I'm not proud of it.

I should have put my wife first. It was always career, then my daughter, then charity work, then rock concerts, and Priyanka was always last.

That's not how a successful marriage works. I'd screwed up and there was no way Priyanka would forgive me. Attractive women don't have to say sorry.

Financially I couldn't afford to move out since the bills on the family home were huge, so we slept in separate rooms and avoided each other.

Hell hath no fury like an Indian woman who gave up her citizenship to be with you.

My depression led to me making a painful visit to my GP. My physical health had deteriorated. I was struggling to walk. While my GP acknowledged the pain of divorce would affect my mental health, I had a scan and discovered osteoarthritis in my right leg, causing me to limp like an old man.

Sleepless nights, limping, prescription drugs to prevent the limping, drugs to help me sleep, drugs to help me cope with the drugs I was taking, nobody to love or talk to, losing my two closest friends who had taken Priyanka's side: I found myself overcome with grief as though a loved one had died. I experienced loud outbursts of crying, followed by shortness of breath and pain in my chest.

I was rushed to hospital, suspecting I was having a heart attack. Thankfully, it was heartburn caused by Indian food.

My parents sided with Priyanka and did everything they could to save the marriage, including an intervention. Mum cried regularly. My in-laws were devastated. I had caused everyone so much pain and felt I was the one at fault.

Getting divorced in the Indian community brings great shame on families. Dad was brutal in his criticism towards me. He'd never run his own business so didn't understand the pressures. He'd never had this kind of marriage problem with Mum. Despite being a brilliant doctor and humanitarian with all the charity work he does at the weekends, there was so much he didn't get about me.

I gave them my suicide letter. It had been written when I knew the marriage was over. It was an accumulation of my feelings about my failure in business, the shame of a man who couldn't support his family, having no money, everything going wrong and being trapped.

Killing yourself is actually difficult. If you drink poison, your body is conditioned to make you vomit to get rid of it.

If you slit your wrists, death won't happen in seconds. It can take hours to bleed out and be brutally painful.

Hanging is only twenty-five per cent successful. They make it look so easy in the movies.

If you jump in front of a train and are run over, this can cause many train drivers to suffer depression and turn to alcohol from shock. I didn't want to do that to anyone.

So, the cliffs at Beachy Head in Sussex were the planned location. They now have chaplains there, to try and stop you from killing yourself. It was a four-hour trip in the car along the M1 and M25, the two worst motorways in the UK, plus the prospect of motorway food which is overpriced, pointless and offers you no happiness.

The thought of the final journey was exhausting, but that was my plan. Driving my car off the Beachy Head cliffs in Sussex.

For the first time in my life, my father's lip wobbled and his eyes filled with tears. I've always looked up to him with a mixture of admiration and fear. It upset me to see him affected like this. He had no idea how bad things had been and said he couldn't imagine what it would be like to lose his son to suicide.

He left the room, made a phone call and returned a moment later with a tissue, wiping away his tears. It was a bonding moment. I asked my father who he'd called.

It was the local Indian restaurant; he was feeling peckish!

A week later, the loneliness still felt unbearable so I joined Match.com, the UK's most popular dating website according to Match.com. It had been over twenty-one years since I was single. I had no idea what the rules were on dating.

Most of the pictures I owned were of me and Priyanka, me and Freya, the three of us or her in-laws. In the few pictures I had of just me, I felt I looked middle-aged and unattractive.

Putting an online dating profile together was difficult, because I couldn't see what other men had written. I had made a mess of my marriage, so clearly hadn't a clue what it was that women wanted (clue: everything), or that a woman's public image on a dating website was often different to their private behaviour, as I would later find out.

"I want a nice kind man" means *"I want someone to treat me badly because, being a woman, I believe I can save men."*

"I want new experiences" means *"I want to try a black man."*

"I'm a nice normal person who can't find Mr Right" means *"I have a drug problem and my ex left me."*

"I'm into normal things like Netflix and music" means *"I'm not going to tell you much about me."*

My head was a mess, so my profile didn't inspire anyone. Here's what I wrote: *"Don't be a psycho like my ex. I've risen to the top, now I'm looking for someone to fall with. If you are not attractive and don't like Bon Jovi, I won't reply."*

Everyone ignored me. Can you blame them?

I paid for a premium package, so was able to see when women looked at my profile. Once they saw my bald head, large nose, enormous ears and bushy eyebrows, they must have thought, *he looks like an Indian Shrek* and moved on to other men's profiles.

When getting divorced, your mind is in turmoil. There's a lot of things you forget to do. The silliest thing I did was not change the computer passwords, so Priyanka saw every message I sent, many blaming her for my pain. More on that later.

I joined Bumble, a dating app where only the woman can approach you. I spent £120 on Bumble coins to get noticed. I was in the spotlights!

Not. A. Single. Woman. Contacted. Me.

When I finally did meet a woman, it was on Plenty of Fish, a less fancy dating site for people often suffering from self-esteem issues. I found myself getting horrific pictures from Northern women over fifty-five and none of them were pictures of their face, if you get my drift. And if you don't, imagine stretched, droopy balloons and strawberries cut in half and left out in the sun.

That's where I met Bilyana. She was a successful psychotherapist from Bulgaria with long dark hair like my wife, kissable lips like my wife, a body that showed she took care of herself, like my wife, and a smile that would disarm anyone and radiated warmth. NOT like my wife.

Bilyana had no idea she was on a seedy website.

Many dating websites sell data to other dating sites without telling anyone. She was horrified when I found her here.

I explained I wasn't like other men and sent her a picture. Bilyana thanked me for not sending a dick pic. Apparently that's what men do?! She said I had a lovely face. We met up. I asked what she was drinking and she told me G & T. Guess what, it was my wife's favourite drink.

As the evening progressed over a candlelit meal, she asked if I was sexually active.

"No, I just lie there," was my answer. It made her laugh and, when Bilyana laughed, her whole body laughed. If you can't be good-looking, be funny. Women seem to like that.

I still didn't see the connection between Bilyana and Priyanka, even when she told me she'd come to England as an immigrant with nothing and built her career from scratch.

Bilyana knew she couldn't have me since I was technically still married. That made her want me even more. Our WhatsApp messages became erotic.

I'd never talked dirty to anyone before and let me tell you this, it was FANTASTIC. Teasing, enticing, tantalising, foreplay, then pure filth …

… and Priyanka saw every SINGLE message on WhatsApp because it was synced from my phone to the family computer.

Priyanka told everyone I was a cheater and a scumbag. That

gave her lots of sympathy. I saw it differently. We were sleeping in separate rooms and getting divorced. I could do what I liked as long as I didn't bring anyone back to the family home.

Unfortunately, most women don't respond to this sort of logic and so everyone turned against me and my parents thought I was an idiot for dating so soon. I needed time to heal. I simply believed I needed a woman to save me. What I needed to do was save myself first. When you're in a hole, unfortunately, you often keep digging.

When Bilyana and I went away for a romantic weekend, Priyanka harassed her in the middle of the night with text messages:

"How do you know Niraj?"

"Did you bring condoms with you?"

"I asked you, how do you know my husband?"

Okay, it's not Shakespeare, but when your phone pings repeatedly at 3 a.m. it has an impact. Priyanka also left inappropriate comments on Bilyana's Facebook business page.

Bilyana quickly broke up with me. She didn't want the drama.

The divorce was now all-out war. The problem was, the more we fought, the more exhausting it became. The only people who benefitted were the solicitors, who spent months negotiating over assets, money and who did what to whom.

I was frustrated, getting nowhere and it was costing me a fortune.

I didn't know how much longer I could last in this state of depression and frustration. All I wanted was to meet someone to have a laugh with, give me a bear hug and share my life with.

I didn't think I was asking for much. As it turned out, I was asking for a lot.

Over the age of forty, it gets tougher to meet the right person. Everyone has emotional baggage. Everyone fears getting hurt. Women would rather chat for months online than actually meet in person.

Dating is complicated. Human beings are complicated and often irrational. How well we carry that emotional baggage is crucial.

With nobody to help or guide me, I only had one mission. To fall in love again. I didn't care what I had to do, how much I had to suffer and how much money I would lose.

Business Lesson Learned

When you repeatedly try and things don't go your way, you have to pivot.

The other option is staying the same, which is the same as failing.

Pivoting isn't easy. Quite often the first pivot doesn't work. You have to try, create new opportunities and ideas, otherwise, you become an awful statistic in businesses that fail. Personal development expert Brian Tracy recommends when times are tough, write down a Top 20 solutions list. The first ten are easy, the last ten are tough and that's usually where your breakthrough exists.

Chapter 6

THINGS GET WORSE BEFORE THEY GET BETTER

After I changed the passwords to my computer, mobile and the cloud, I decided to go old school and try speed dating. My generation prefers meeting people face to face rather than online. After all, people over forty didn't grow up with the internet. We're not as addicted and can switch off from time to time, unlike the younger generation who treat the internet like it's their last day on earth.

What surprised me was that most speed-dating events in London were for those aged between twenty-one and thirty or between thirty and forty-five. Only ten per cent of events were for over-forty-fives!

All the pictures on the websites were of young happy people. Nobody of my age. There were also variations, like Jenga-themed parties, where you have to play board games to break the ice, or Lock and Key, where you search for a lock that fits the key.

On *Date in a Dash,* one of the organisers kept referring to everyone as sexy singles, dishy guys and gorgeous girls. What an exciting world to thrive in!

I didn't want anything gimmicky. I just wanted to meet someone I could talk to and connect with.

Speed-dating events advertised hundreds of people in attendance, all glamorous pictures of happy, smiling faces.

Imagine my horror when I paid money for my first ever speed-dating event. I can't even remember the name of the company. I walked down narrow steep stairs and into the tiny basement of a bar in Wardour Street in central London. It was about the size of my kitchen. I observed ten women sitting down at ten different tables, and twelve men awkwardly standing at the bar with their backs to the women.

No glamour or glitz going on here.

At forty-seven, I was the youngest person there. The men were roughly fifty to sixty years of age and so were the women.

It was a typical London scenario. People don't talk on the underground. Strangers in London rarely meet. This was no exception. You could have heard a pin drop. People stared at their mobile phones or alcohol glasses like nobody wanted to be there.

The men avoided eye contact. Some nodded then sized each other up, leaning against the bar. Most were dressed in ties and suits and had come straight from work judging by their briefcases and manbags. When I was little, my mother would give me Brussels sprouts and aubergines. I would make a face like it was the worst experience I'd ever had. These men were making the same face.

I decided to stand out by not wearing a suit. I wore a perfectly ironed white shirt, blue jeans, polished brown shoes and a jacket with a handkerchief in the top pocket, giving me the entrepreneur look. As it was, I didn't need this outfit to stand out. I was the only person of colour. I know Indians have relatives to introduce them, but what do Asians and Africans do? Why were they not here? How were they meeting people?

It was made worse when two women walked into the room as the event was about to start, glanced at me and the other men and quickly left. We could hear the clatter of their footsteps up the hard stairs.

Speed-dating companies promise to make you feel welcome and help you to mingle. Yes, they said hello as you walked in, but that was it. Nobody made an effort to make us comfortable, ask how we were feeling or tell us not to worry.

You're given a scorecard where you tick Y or N. If the women ticked Y and so did you, they were sent your details. If the women ticked N, you couldn't contact them. So at least the companies took the women's privacy into consideration.

Because there were two extra men, there were always two men standing at the bar, ill at ease, waiting to meet a woman. This is how it worked:

"You have three minutes to talk to a woman, then you move to the next table. You will know it's three minutes because a bell will sound." Our host held up the bell like none of us knew what a bell was and shook it like none of us had ever heard a bell ring before. "You're not meant to exchange numbers or business cards. Everyone goes through us for your own personal safety. Be nice, have fun and good luck."

My heart was racing and my legs were wobbling. I talk to people all the time in business with ease, from the assistant to the manager. With CEOs it can be tricky, since many play mind games and are in positions of great power, but overall, I can hold my own. For some reason, this was more nerve-wracking.

It was like the first day of high school. Unfortunately, when I get nervous I sweat and it all starts with my egg-shaped forehead.

"Hi, how am I, how are you?" I blurted out.

"Don't worry, I don't want to be here either," said Bailey, with a welcoming smile. She was late fifties with bags under her eyes and hair with a LOT of clips.

"This is my first time. Is this your first time?"

"The twenty-second," she said, popping an olive from her martini into her mouth.

"You've done this twenty-two times? How? Why?"

"My father worked on a farm. I've seen animals go to slaughter and they're treated with more humanity than online dating, so I swore I'd never go back."

I didn't know how to react to that. She'd sucked the happiness out of the air.

"So, are you vegan?"

Bailey looked at me like I was thick. Then she removed her mobile and for the next two and a half minutes replied to messages. She hadn't turned her sound off, so I could hear the clicking of every key while everybody else was chatting.

The bell rang. Thank God for that. I reached into my pocket for a tissue to stop my dripping forehead and didn't have one. So I took the nearest thing I could find – the coaster – and scraped the perspiration from my forehead like a Neanderthal. If I had shaving foam, it would look like I was shaving my head.

I got up and moved onto the next table. Daisy was early sixties with crooked teeth. She looked more like a grandmother sipping on her brandy than a woman searching for love. She was nervously friendly. "Hello. So nice to meet you. Indian food is my favourite!"

I didn't recall asking what food she liked or ate.

"Chicken tikka. The nation's favourite!" she added.

She wasn't being rude or condescending. Whenever white English people are awkward around Indians, they talk about chicken tikka, *Goodness Gracious Me* or Gandhi in the first sixty seconds. There's no reason to be awkward. We bleed like everybody else.

"Have you seen the TV show *Goodness Gracious Me*?" she asked.

"Yes, my cousins starred in it," I said, in a clearly sarcastic voice.

"Tell them they were good."

Be calm, Niraj, I repeated in my head.

"Wasn't Mahatma Gandhi a wonderful man?" she asked. "The way he changed India and made the world a better place. Bravo, Matty. Bravo."

Did she just give a nickname to one of the world's greatest leaders?

"There's 1.5 billion Indians in the world," I said. "I don't know all of them! Can we talk about something else, like, I don't know ... maybe just talk to me like a human being and not a person of colour?" I felt bad for raising my voice, but sometimes it has to be done to get your point across.

Daisy didn't seem ashamed or shocked, merely surprised. She picked up her pen and ticked N, followed by a disapproving "humph".

I'd gone from being rejected in twenty seconds to being rejected in thirty seconds. On the plus side, I was improving.

Elaine had long curly hair, more make-up than was necessary and a pink dress. She added pink lipstick as I sat down.

"Could I have some?" I said, trying to break the tension.

"It's not hygienic," replied Elaine, unaware of my humour.

I wanted to change the conversation and make it more interesting. "So if there was a movie made about you, which actor would play the starring role?" I asked, genuinely curious.

"No idea," Elaine replied immediately.

Really. Not even a thought. Don't give up, Niraj. Keep going ...

"Where's your favourite holiday destination ever?" I asked.

"Peterborough."

One-word answers are death to conversation, and why choose Peterborough? It was voted the worst place to live in the UK.

"What kind of men do you like?"

"I'd rather not say," she replied.

Four words. I was getting better at this.

"We're in London," I said. "I'm not going to judge you."

"I like men who ..." she began.

I made hand gestures, encouraging her.

"... don't look like you."

That knocked me down a peg. At least I couldn't go any lower.

"It's not a race thing," she added. "I just prefer white men."

I stood corrected. Down another peg.

"Okay, well, if you'll excuse me, I'm going to kill myself," I said.

I went to the men's toilet to grab some toilet roll. The sweat had gone from my forehead to other parts of my body I'd rather not mention. I was surprised to see three men who looked familiar. None of them were using the urinals, they just didn't want to be speed dating.

"Just to clarify – none of you have had it as bad as me," I said to them.

For the first time, the men displayed some energy. We spoke over each other in our haste to prove who had had the worst time.

"She's drunk," said Man One in a double-breasted jacket. He had wavy hair and a bulbous nose. It wasn't as red as Rudolph's but not far off.

"Desperate," said Man Two in a plain black suit, unkempt hair with glasses at the end of his nose.

"She's both," said Man Three in a pinstriped suit. He looked like your typical tall city banker. "Why is it so difficult to meet the right woman? I haven't even mentioned my criminal record or substance abuse."

"I'm buying the first round," I said. "We can spend all night talking about women and drown our sorrows. Who's with me?"

All three men showed disapproval and left. I was tempted to follow. However, I would never want anyone to walk out on me if I had made the effort to get ready for a date. The bell rang and I went out to try again, armed with layers of toilet roll in my pocket, should I sweat any more.

After meeting six more women, I was exhausted. I'd only been here for twenty-seven minutes and it felt like an eternity. I forgot their names and what they did. I just wanted it to be over.

By the time I got to Woman Ten, we both looked miserable. We sighed heavily in unison.

"I'm glad I'm not the only one," smiled Gill, a petite lady with cropped hair, blue eyes and a pearl necklace.

"Lovely necklace," I said, being genuine.

"My nana gave it to me," she replied.

"I lived with my grandmother for years. Miss her every day."

"I miss my nana too."

That was it. We smiled. Our eyes met. She reached out and held my hand. "Why is it so difficult to find the right person?"

"Don't ask me. I'm worse than a hopeless romantic, I'm a hopeful one," I said.

Gill laughed. A proper laugh. Right from her gut. "You're the only man who's made me smile all evening."

"Wait till you see me naked!" Don't know why I said that.

Gill laughed again. She was sipping on orange juice and I couldn't smell any booze on her breath. This looked promising.

"So there's no misunderstanding," I said. "Please confirm you're not a vegetarian, condescending, racist or just annoying."

"Good questions are a sign of intelligence," she replied.

"Thank you, kind lady."

"Especially when asked if I'm a racist."

"More of a precautionary measure," I said.

"I confirm that, your honour."

"You confirm that you're a racist?"

Gill quickly wanted to explain. I playfully stopped her by holding up my hands. "No worries, so am I. The best part is that nobody suspects because I'm Indian."

"Congratulations. You've passed my test."

Gill was almost jumping out of her seat. "*I've* passed *your* test? How about you pass mine?"

My confidence had grown and I proudly delineated my hot, chubby body. "Just look at me! You're welcome."

Gill rested her hand on her shoulder and stared at me. It was refreshing and made me feel like I mattered.

"Would you like to have a cup of tea with me sometime?" she asked.

"On one condition," I said.

"Anything," she said, smiling.

"What's your name?"

"I just asked a man out and I didn't know his name. Just to let you know that's not usually me."

"Dating over forty makes you do unusual things. I look forward to knowing the real you." I handed her my phone and she typed in her name and number.

That was the best three minutes I'd ever had without sex.

This is what dating should be like. Fun, exciting, sexy, thrilling. Not two people who would rather be somewhere else exchanging CVs over an Italian meal.

They say you should wait two days before calling a woman. Two minutes after I'd left the bar I did everything I could not to call Gill. I thanked God, walked fast, listened to rock music, grabbed a burger on the way home. Nothing worked.

I didn't think I'd meet anyone so soon after Bilyana broke up with me.

Calling Gill so soon would be too desperate. I didn't want to seem needy. At the same time, I wanted her to know I was thinking about her.

Hi Gill, had an amazing time with you tonight. Text me when you get home safe. x

Who is this? came the quick reply.

You joker. It's Niraj, from speed dating.

Got the wrong number, mate.

What? No! That wasn't possible.

Gill, quit goofing around. I replied. *We met at the very end.*

We got on like a house on fire and we were meant to be ...

I deleted the last sentence before sending.

Sorry. Not Gill.

She must have given me the wrong number. The next day I called the speed-dating company and explained the misunderstanding. Could they please call Gill and get her to give me the correct phone number? They checked the scoring card. Gill had ticked N.

"That doesn't make sense. Why would she be nice to me and give her number?"

"You're not meant to exchange numbers," the man reminded me. "That's against the rules."

"Sod the rules. Why would she lie to me like that?"

"That's a loaded question," came the reply. "Sometimes women don't want to say no in case it hurts your feelings."

"She was the real deal," I assured him. "Women don't fake ..." I'm glad I didn't finish that sentence. "She was genuine. I thought she liked me."

"If I had a tenner for every time a man said that I'd be living it up in Monaco. Why don't you sign up for our next speed-dating event? You have to get back on the horse!"

"I've had enough of horses. I want a golden retriever. A goddamn golden retriever!" I nearly choked on my words.

I hung up and threw my phone across the room, smashing the screen.

Why would Gill waste my time and hurt my feelings?

Is this why men have drinking problems?

Is this why painful love songs are so famous because we all have to deal with this kind of nonsense?

I didn't know. I'd never had a period of dating.

In high school, I'd had one girlfriend. Julie Monaghan was a blonde bombshell, like a busty fifteen-year-old Marilyn Monroe. Everyone was scared to ask her out because she was so attractive. Boys would either be struck dumb or show off around her. I talked to her about classical music: she played violin, I played kettle drums. I asked her out and she said yes. We lasted five months. In teenage years, that's like five years.

I thought she was the love of my life. The other girls at school couldn't understand why Julie would date a Paki. Some girls told her she could catch AIDS or become brown herself if we slept together.

Small-town Northern Ireland wasn't the brightest place to grow up.

This made our relationship stronger. If we could withstand the high school crowd, we could achieve anything. We lasted five months until the unthinkable happened.

Everyone at school was staring at me and whispering behind my back more than usual. I asked what was going on and nobody would tell me. As I left school, I found a note in my schoolbag: *Julie snogged Alan Simpson in the back of the bus. Sorry. Anonymousse.*

Yes, that was how they spelt anonymous.

Julie denied it. It was on the bus on the way back from the ice-skating rink. Everyone at school was on there, so cheating on me in public would be foolish. I knew it was true when the racist scumbags at my school told me, "What she did was cruel and out of order." Imagine that. Then Julie admitted it.

I was so demoralised by what happened, I didn't have another girlfriend for six years. When I did, it was the fabulous

Ann from Northern Ireland. We met in England when I was trying to become a rock star. She was a skinny brunette who always smiled and had a special gift; everyone felt comfortable around her. She never criticised, never blamed, never judged, always came from a place of love.

I can't be with a skinny woman. After all, I'm a large man. When they stand next to me, I look gargantuan.

I was in A & E, waiting for medication for my throat. I had been singing all day and had lost my voice. Ann pulled back the curtains of the dull, depressing National Health Service hospital, which reeked of bleach as most NHS hospitals do.

I told her my life story and she said she'd always wanted to date a rock star. She was bored of dating intelligent, educated men and wanted something different.

We had three glorious months. We swore we'd always be together. Every single night. It was the simple things: takeaway and TV. Dinner and a movie. Then her placement at the A & E finished and she returned to Dungannon in Northern Ireland, a town about forty-five minutes west of Belfast, where everyone sounds like a friendly farmer. In other words, the Irish version of Bristol.

I promised to write letters and stay in touch. She believed in me as a songwriter and was the only person who would tell me I had great talent.

Despite this, Ann never wrote back or spoke to me once she went back home. One day I called her home and her mother answered.

That was back in the days when you would talk to the woman's parents first and not even address them by their first names. It would be, "Hi, Mrs Doris," or "Hello, Mr Doris." You would chat for at least thirty seconds before asking to speak to their daughter.

I would walk ten minutes to the nearest payphone in the bitter January wind, since there were no mobiles in those days. You didn't want to go anywhere in London after dark. Ann would finish her shift around 10 p.m. or midnight at the hospital, and I would leave my flat armed with my umbrella – because when gangs attack you with knives, we all know how helpful umbrellas are.

When she never replied, it hurt even more, since I had no friends or family in London.

All the record companies had rejected me. Sony Music Entertainment UK were my last chance for success. They said no by letter. It was the standard nonsense: "You're not what we're looking for." That's why there's so many failed singers out there. Nobody tells you where you're going wrong.

I needed to hear Ann's voice. I needed someone to listen and help me deal with all the failure I was enduring.

Mrs Doris said, "If my Ann is interested, she will call you."

I never heard from her again.

Over the years I've googled her in Dungannon, Northern Ireland and checked Facebook. No idea where she is, who she's married to or where she went.

Back to the present. Love was eluding me and my divorce was making me question if I'd ever find happiness again.

Business Lesson Learned

Things often get worse before they get better. You don't often see it at the time, you think you're making a bad decision. That's because you have no idea what the outcome will be and you're terrified of failing.

It's vital to jump out of your comfort zone to try something new. Change is terrifying and hard work, which is why most people can't change. It may not go as you planned. That's okay. It's part of the journey.

Focus on the process and what you learn, not the end result. Most of all, do everything with a positive mindset and calm mind. You make better decisions that way.

Chapter 7

ASK FOR HELP

Things had become so unbearable at home between me and Priyanka that I moved out of the family home on Christmas Eve. I needed time to think clearly and if we were together over Christmas, my mind would continue to be a mess.

While searching for love, I was also battling mental health issues.

According to the Samaritans, a charity I have donated to for several years, the suicide rate is highest among men between the ages of forty-five and forty-nine. That didn't fill me with confidence. Drinking myself into insanity wouldn't help. Drugs are never the solution. I needed a hit of something.

Hope.

Someone to talk to. Someone who would listen to my problems. Someone to hold my hand and tell me it would be okay. When you're trapped, you often can't find a way out. I wrote down ideas, meditated and went for walks; nothing worked.

To make matters worse, I couldn't find anywhere to live. No estate agent would rent a flat to me for less than six months, yet I only needed one for two months until my new house was ready. I offered to pay more rent for a two-month lease and no estate agents would accept it.

So I went off book and found a one-bedroom flat on a rundown estate in Winslow, a small town about twenty miles from Milton Keynes. The high street had cheap takeaways, a Co-op and several homeless loitering about at night.

Moving from a luxurious family home to a one-bedder in the middle of nowhere was a punch to the throat. I'd delivered LinkedIn training that morning to a local business, so I had my business suit on and a Waitrose bag of bread, beans, coffee, a saucepan and utensils.

Due to my ill health from the depression, my GP advised me against lifting anything heavy or being under too much stress. I looked a right prima donna as I arrived, with the workmen carrying everything and me in a business suit carrying only a Waitrose shopping bag.

Children peeked out the curtains. At 3 p.m., it was almost dark and the winter rain was pelting outside. The house was so small it took three attempts for the movers to get my bed inside the front door. I'd left my TV in storage since I was convinced it would get stolen. Just as well, it would barely have fitted in the living room.

I paid the workmen, noticing that not only were there kids staring, but their bored jobless parents had joined in. I scowled and put on my toughest look. I did a slow strut towards their house, warning them to stay away from me. I was a force to be reckoned with, a man from the streets of Belfast, a man who understood the real meaning of terror growing up … and then slipped on muddy grass and fell on my backside.

I could hear howls of laughter from all directions from inside the houses. I was staring at the sky, my bum cheeks were hurting and the rain was hitting my face. I didn't move for a minute. A door opened and I heard footsteps thundering in my direction.

A double-chinned lady helped me up, told me I looked like shit – and yes, she did sound like Ray Winstone. I didn't say anything. She thought I was a newly arrived immigrant and spoke very slowly, over-pronouncing every word.

"Would you like a cup of tea?" she asked, with genuine concern.

"I'm fine thanks, don't worry about it," I replied in my Irish accent.

"Oh my God!" she shrieked. "You're American! Hey kids, he's American!"

I didn't have the strength to correct her. Two boys with crew cuts rushed out, seven and eight years old. They stood over me.

"Do you know the Avengers?" asked the youngest.

"Have you been to Disneyland?" asked the eldest.

"What brings you here?" asked their mum.

"The Devil!" I replied as I struggled up. "We have unfinished business …" Don't know why I said that.

Her friendliness disappeared. She rushed back inside with her kids. I heard them lock the front door.

The heating system in the one-bedder was decades old. The manual made less sense than an IKEA instruction leaflet. I got out of my dirty clothes and put on my T-shirt, shirt, jumper, long overcoat (with massive holes and rips) and my scarf.

It was like being in North India in December 1997. I had come full circle. Nothing had changed. I was doomed to a life of loneliness.

I figured I would work through Christmas. If reality wasn't working, living in denial was the next best option. I had my second sales book to finish. That would be my priority.

I didn't get a wink of sleep all night because I was in a new place, plus the front door shook constantly from the howling wind. I started the day with a scream as the cold shower pounded my face. The heating still wasn't working. This was not how I'd planned to spend Christmas Day.

No family, no kids, no wife: the flat echoed with emptiness. I had baked beans, toast and a coffee for breakfast. There was no fancy milk frother, so I planned to shake the carton of soya milk until I had no feeling left in my arms.

I opened the fridge and the unsweetened soya milk had leaked everywhere.

"There's children in this world with no food. Be grateful," I told myself, though I desperately needed a caffeine fix. Brutally strong black coffee it was.

I got stuck into my book around 8 a.m., wrote about 2,000 words and at lunchtime went for a walk. It was so quiet. Not many cars were in the parking area. *Maybe they had been stolen overnight,* I thought cynically.

'Twas the season to wish one another joy and love and peace on earth.

Except I didn't see a single person. No leaves on the trees, no love in the air, not even any stray dogs to pet. I walked past houses. Out of the corner of my eye I glimpsed Christmas tree lights. I could hear crackers pop. I slowed down as I went past living-room windows, staring at the life I'd once had.

Some families were still in pyjamas. Some had three generations in their ranks. I stopped and stared, wishing that was me. A grandmother caught me gazing wistfully and mouthed "Fuck off". So much for Christmas spirit.

I quickly went back to my one-bedder and had beans on toast again for my lunch. I went to switch on the TV so at least there was noise in the house – then I remembered I didn't have one. I'd grown up enjoying James Bond movies and Morecambe and Wise Christmas specials plus the ultimate Christmas lunch from my mother – Indian food. Even on Christmas Day, my father didn't want change. Life had seemed so amazing then.

My head became filled with negative thoughts. I couldn't think straight. I felt like my insides had been taken out.

The walls closed in. My breathing got faster and sharper. I was freaking out. I put a post on Twitter about feeling lonely on Christmas Day. Usually on Twitter, I get a like or two. This time I got thirty-nine likes and a retweet.

It was great for a momentary high, except nobody called me and nobody hugged me. We're all connected by technology yet we've never been so alone.

I wanted someone to talk to, laugh with, kiss, make love to and have dinner with.

I had a meltdown, stamping my feet on the hard floor and smacking my head like I was losing my mind. The flat was so flimsy the lights on the wall shook. I was determined not to cry. My body shuddered. I cried hard like I was at the funeral of a best friend. There's no nice way to say it. Depression is a fucker. An uncontrollable devil that takes pleasure from your worst nightmares.

Everyone talks about the battle against drugs and alcohol. I've battled alcohol addiction as a teenager. I quit smoking after ten years. I've been kicked down so many times and always found the strength to get back up. Nothing has ever slammed me as hard as divorce.

I didn't know what to do or who to turn to. I wanted to call Freya, but felt ashamed asking my daughter for help.

After nervously taking several sleeping tablets, I went to sleep. Sometimes, a good night's sleep can cure you of all ills. When I woke up twelve hours later, it was Boxing Day.

My head was pounding. My body was in pain as I struggled out of bed. Somehow, I felt grateful to be alive. Not so grateful that I could smile.

I always keep a glass of water by my bedside table, a habit I picked up from my mother. I gulped it down feeling thirsty. Staring hard in the bathroom mirror, I didn't like what I saw. No hair where I wanted hair and too much hair where I didn't need it. The tiniest of hairs on my head were grey, not luxuriant silver fox, but grey, like my grandfather's pubes – don't ask me how I know that.

My double chin wobbled as I moved my jaw up and down.

My man boobs were drooping more than they should. If anyone had squeezed them, I'd have been worried they might have made a honking sound.

You could have hung a washing line of clothes on my love handles.

I wished I could change how I looked. Everything except …

… my legs and ass, those I was proud of. No matter how out of shape I got, I maintained my sprinter's legs. Even osteo-arthritis didn't make them look bad. No idea how or why, and yes, it looked weird. Like I'd stolen somebody else's legs and was wearing them. They were so out of sync with the rest of my body.

After the age of forty, your looks start to fade unless you're a model, or able to afford the most expensive lotions, potions, treatments and procedures. You can no longer eat the food you once did and have to watch your weight. It's a quite simple rule when eating: if it tastes bad, like porridge, berries or kale, it's good for you. If it tastes good, like kebabs, fish and chips, Jaffa cakes sandwiched in between digestive biscuits – yes, that's a thing – then it's bad for you.

You get out of bed in the morning. This will be followed by "Oh, dear" or worse, like you're lifting weights.

The clothes you once wore don't fit as well, especially around the waist.

I had two choices. I could waste the rest of my Christmas wallowing in bitterness and self-pity, which was tempting, or I could try and move forward with my life. So I reluctantly put together a new dating profile. Despite my loneliness and emotionally unstable state, I was ready get back out there. This is what it said:

I enjoy Love Actually, Mamma Mia and The Holiday. I'm a lovely guy who has been hurt. I will never hurt you.

I don't want to say today's music is shit and young people don't know what good music is, but today's music is shit and young people don't know what good music is.

I'm not into one-night stands but won't object if you prefer that.

Since women like humour, I ended with "*I'm not into one-night stands but won't object if you prefer that*" and, yes, I actually added the ha at the end to signify laughter.

Why did the man cross the road? He heard the chicken was a slut.

Ha.

I couldn't go through with it. Thank God, judging by how awful my profile was.

I spoke to the one woman I had a connection with – my

mum. It started with the usual "Hi, how are you? Merry Christmas" then I said nothing. Mum asked what was wrong. She knew her eldest well. Sniffling was heard down the phone, telling her how lonely I was. I can't imagine how bad I would feel if my daughter was broken-hearted and struggling in her life. Mum immediately sent me a ticket to fly over to Northern Ireland. I spent the rest of that Christmas with my parents, sister, brother and adorable nephews.

Being with my family was a joy. I revelled in the familiarity and this gave me the confidence to think more positively and clearly. We went for walks and it rained. Indian families turned up unannounced expecting food. Neighbours popped in to say hello. They guzzled Mum's fruit trifle, which was perfect soul food. Dad ordered takeaway pizza on Saturday night like he had done for twenty years.

When the pizza parlour asked his name he would reply, "Dr Kapur FRCP, Fellow of the Royal College of Surgeons and MBE from Prince Charles (now King Charles)." This was always followed by a pause, since it sounded like someone was taking the piss. He wasn't. He was deadly serious.

When I returned to my awful flat on New Year's Eve, I could feel the walls closing in. There was nobody to talk to. Isolation and loneliness were horrible room-mates. I don't know how the elderly cope. Going for days with nobody to talk to, abandoned and left uncared for. My situation was no different. At least I was able to fly back home to see everyone for a few days. That meant something.

I hired former European lightweight boxing champion Billy Schwer to do mindset coaching with me to sort my head out. He'd been a legend in his prime and was now a legendary personal coach, "inspiring and empowering people to live with passion, power and purpose", according to his website.

Billy and I had spoken at a sales conference several months earlier that had been organised by my friend, Mia Butler. There was mutual respect between Billy and I, although I thought he was way better at speaking. My style was rehearsed and refined, but Billy's was raw and unrehearsed, yet also emotional and uplifting. I'm so glad he spent weeks training me up to be a normal human being again … or as normal as you can be in this digital day and age.

"Self-pity is bollocks, Niraj. You're a beautiful man. You did the best you could in the circumstances. Bilyana, she wasn't for you. Alice wasn't for you. (*I'd met Alice at a networking event, but every time I asked her out, she kept trying to sell me Arbornne products.*) Naomi wasn't for you. (*I'd met Naomi at a different business networking event. We'd had chemistry, she'd given me her number and agreed to go to the theatre with me. Never heard from her again. Phone calls and texts were not returned.*) This is your time! I believe in you! Now go get it!" Billy would tell me daily in his working-class Luton accent, and yes, he sounded like Ray Winstone.

That's why you should always be kind to people, especially those who are not paying attention to what you say or dismissive of you. Everyone is fighting an internal battle you know nothing about – and a kind word or gesture can make all the difference. I really needed Billy's support.

On Valentine's Day – the worst day of the year for lonely people – the shops were full of over-the-top romantic gestures and money-making sentimentality. Priyanka used to say she didn't care about Valentine's Day. She wanted to be treated well the other 364 days of the year.

So I rebelled by moving house on Valentine's Day. The tenants left earlier than expected and at last I had my own place. Four bedrooms, large windows, in a middle-class cul-de-sac in a safe part of Milton Keynes. I didn't see my elderly white neighbours in autumn or winter. They would pop up in the spring to say good morning. In the summer they talked about the weather like they were professional weather people.

The house was too big for one person. The plan was that I would get it done up and rent out two rooms and a bathroom. The extra money, after the mortgage payment, would be £700 a month. That would help Freya through university, and I would have people in the house to keep me company.

With my increased confidence and more sales coaching clients hiring me to deliver LinkedIn training and guidance sessions on overcoming objections, prospecting and email writing, I started earning decent money again. I had work lined up until June. So I hired painters and handymen to get the house done up.

I was convinced 2020 was going to be my year. What would possibly go wrong?

As a coach, I tell my clients that when you get rejected, don't mope around or waste time feeling sorry for yourself. Business is a numbers game. Get out there and try again.

Business Lesson Learned

Ask for help. We all struggle from time to time. It's okay to feel lonely. It's okay to be lost. It's not okay to do nothing about it, otherwise you will never grow, develop or progress. There's never any shame in asking for help, especially for men who would rather drink themselves into a stupor than ask for help.

When you ask for help, you get a new perspective, often a new idea. It's never a sign of weakness, in fact it takes courage to ask for help.

It's not a sign of weakness to ask for help if you're new or struggling. If you've been in business for decades, it's still a smart idea to ask for help. It doesn't matter if the person you ask is famous or an influencer.

All that matters is "Do they care?" and "Can they help?" If they're a nice person, it's a bonus.

Chapter 8

FOCUS

While my house was being redecorated, I was hired to sales-train ten people at an industrial estate in Hampshire. They worked in storage and had no idea how to create a sales funnel or upsell a customer from simple storage to a man with a van and storage insurance without sounding like terrible salespeople.

Enter Niraj.

It was a two-hour drive from my house, and in morning traffic, you don't want to be anywhere near the M1 and M25. So I stayed overnight in a local hotel. Hotel food is bland and over-priced, much like food in airports, airplanes and service stations in the UK.

Though I grew up with a vegetarian family, was married to a vegetarian and, yes, even my daughter is a veggie, I enjoy eating meat on the road since I don't know how to cook it.

The burger bun was stodgy. The lettuce was limp. The chips tasted awful and there were so few of them!

Luckily, midweek football was on and I enjoyed watching Liverpool, a team who have been denied the Premier League title for thirty years. They were playing majestic football once again.

"Bleurgh!" I said, as I stopped eating the terrible food.

Morgan was watching the game. She didn't look like the football fans I have met. I rarely see women at games unless it's England at an international game. She wore a little black dress with boots, had fine cheekbones and drank a pint of cider.

"Cheer up. We're going to win the league this year!" she said.

"When I was growing up, they had Dalglish, Souness, Hansen … the greatest footballers of their generation. Losing was impossible," I replied.

"I've met Bruce Grobbelaar."

"Me too!" I said, perking up. "He's so …"

"Funny," we said at the same time.

That was all we needed. Morgan grabbed a seat beside me and straddled the chair. Her blonde hair shimmered as she moved. She had open body language and focused on me and me only.

We talked about the history of Liverpool Football Club, the greatest goals they had ever scored, their fall from grace after Manchester United took over with Alex Ferguson as their manager and their ascension back to the top. I could feel the eyes of a few locals staring at me with jealousy. Stare all you want. I was happy.

Two ciders and a Diet Coke later, the match had finished and people were leaving.

"What was the score?" asked Morgan.

"Play your cards right, maybe you'll score tonight," I replied.

Morgan reacted as any normal woman would, hearing a corny line – by mocking my appalling pickup techniques.

"Does that actually work on women?"

"I'm seriously out of practice. I'm so sorry."

"Don't be. You're scoring tonight. Start your engines, lover-boy."

"I beg your pardon?"

Dating should be done slowly and with care. Romance, courtship, foreplay is all part of the game of love. However, when you've been alone a long time, you're grateful for anything that comes your way.

The car park was full of taxis taking fans home and designated drivers taking their friends home. I stood there thinking of options. "My hotel is five minutes away," I said.

She ripped off my jacket, threw it on the floor and dragged me into a dark alley. Well, normally it would be dark, but with all the cars and headlights in the car park, people could see us when they walked by and a curious few were having a peek.

Morgan unbuttoned my shirt. I was nervous. "People can see us!"

"That's all part of the fun," she replied with a naughty glint in her eye.

Morgan unbuckled my belt, pulled my zip down and pulled out my … "Wait, hang on, you're drunk and I'm a gentleman," I said. "I will never take advantage!"

"I'm not drunk," she replied. "Two ciders is called Wednesday night!"

"So you're an … exhibitionist?"

Morgan ignored me and removed her panties.

I zipped up my trousers. "Stop this nonsense. We're British." I buckled my belt. "You can have any man, why me?"

"Ugly men make more effort." She pulled up her panties.

I was hurt that she thought of me as ugly. I wanted sex, but not like this. Call me old-fashioned, but I have to have a bed or a sofa. At least somewhere where strangers are not observing my every love handle. I put on my jacket. It was the first time in my life I had turned down sex – not that I had that many options to choose from in the first place.

"You're sick and you need help," I warned her. "If you don't get help, you will self-destruct."

Morgan was humiliated, so decided to turn the tables on me. "Help! Mugger!" she shouted.

People heard her. A taxi driver flung open his car door and got out.

Two other men scrambled out of their car.

"That illegal immigrant has my money!" Morgan told them.

I gave her a dirty look. She gave me the finger. Then I ran away while three semi-drunk men charged after me. One of them shouted "Al-Qaeda!"

I've never known members of Al-Qaeda to be clean-shaven and wear tailored business suits, but that's a conversation for another time.

Despite my weight now, I was a sprinter until the age of sixteen and trained with the Northern Ireland Athletics team. They're one of the worst athletic teams in the world, but that's not the point. My personal best was 12.02 seconds and I was ranked no. 2 at my school in the 100m sprint and no. 1 in the 4 x 100m relay team. If you're under 11 seconds, you have a chance at the Olympics.

For the first few hundred metres, the Hampshire locals are behind me like they're hunting a criminal. At a certain age, your body doesn't quite move as you want it to. I'd had a burger, chips and Diet Coke for dinner, so I got a stitch in my sides – while the crazies who thought I was a mugger caught up with me.

Fear kept me going all the way back to the hotel. I ran into Reception, hit the elevator button and closed the door. I was pressing it insanely as the maniacs closed in on me, yelling, "Oi! Randy Gandhi!"

Quite how I went from "turning down a woman for sex" to "illegal terrorist immigrant on the run" was beyond me. I got off at floor three of the hotel, but could hear my pursuers running up the stairs, yelling comments on Brexit. I dashed to my room and flashed my key card; it wouldn't open.

Why do we have key cards for doors? The bastards never work when you want them to. I heard the emergency door open with a bang. I flashed my key card again. The door light turned green. I opened it and locked it behind me. I could hear footsteps running by as they speculated on what room I could be in.

Sweat was dripping off me. My heart was pounding and I was terrified they would give a description to the manager, who would recognise me. How many Indian Irishmen stay in remote hotels in Hampshire? Answer: one, me.

I moved away from the door and locked myself in the bathroom. Every minute felt like an eternity. Sometime later, I cautiously peeked out of the hotel window. They had gone. No commotion. No police. No press. I was okay … or so I thought.

The next day I met Keith, the owner of the storage company. He was an obese, cheerful Brummie in a shirt and jumper. "Your LinkedIn posts are the best. So excited to have the team working with you, Niraj. They need you to give them a push. My wife, Cynthia, is the ops director. She's shy, so please be patient," he said.

"I'll get your team up and running by end of the day," I

told him. I made that promise to every client and I always kept my word.

The team entered: sales executives, account managers, admin staff, office manager. Early twenties to late thirties everyday people.

In any room where I have to train people:

Three people genuinely want to learn how to make more sales, because it's a tough profession full of daily rejection. One of them is usually the boss.

Two people glance discreetly at their mobile, some even text. They drop a pen on the floor, apologise and reply quickly to texts under the desk.

Two people are secretly looking for jobs at night, so don't want to be there, but play along.

One person always thinks they know everything and is a pain in the neck.

One person fights sleep from boredom due to a late one the previous night.

One person is hard to read. They're soft then loud, passive then aggressive, sweet then annoying. That person walked in the room, gorgeous in her long skirt, glasses, with her shimmering blonde hair tied back … Jesus H. It was Morgan from last night. "We haven't met before, I'm Cynthia," she said.

I extended my hand and she gave me a limp handshake.

Cynthia sat at the back of the room with Keith. Demure and sweet. Was this an act or was she winding me up?

Most trainers work with PowerPoint or handouts. These are terrible ways to learn. The most effective way for people to improve is to make the session interactive, writing answers on a whiteboard or a flip chart. Most trainers avoid this because it's hard work. My job is to get my clients results, so I'll do the hard work instead of taking the easy option. Teaching this way and asking them all to commit to three things is how I get results.

"What is sales? Cynthia?" I asked.

"Oh, gosh. I don't know. Trust?" said Cynthia innocently. "Without trust, you have nothing."

"Well said, petal," Keith murmured.

"Yes, trust is vital," I said. "When people break your trust, how can you work with them?" She was giving nothing away. "No? Anyone else?"

Eddie, a young go-getter with puffy cheeks, shot his hand up, revealing a fancy watch that you see featured in the back of lifestyle magazines. "Confidence."

"Yes, confidence is a good one …"

Cynthia sat demurely and politely with her legs crossed.

I fumbled, mumbled and lost my concentration many times.

The morning session was over. Everyone politely thanked me and left – apart from Keith and Cynthia.

"Keith, could I have a word before you go?" I asked.

Morgan shook her head no, but I wanted to tell him. He had a right to know. It would ruin the chances of me ever being hired by him again, but I had to tell him. Dating was horrible, full of people with bad intentions and I didn't want Keith getting hurt.

"Last night at The Old Crown pub, there was a … kerfuffle," I said.

"Cynthia told me," Keith said. "A terrorist was on the loose."

"Yes, accurate reporting. Well, your Cynthia is actually Morgan and she seduced me in the parking lot. I know this is devastating for you, but you have to know …"

Keith appeared confused then turned to her calmly. "What happened to Giselle?"

"I was so bored of being Giselle," Cynthia said, smirking.

Say what now?

"You know about this?" I asked Keith, dumbfounded.

"When you've been married a long time, you have to keep things fresh," he said.

"But she … you know … back alley action!"

"It's not that sordid," said Keith, cheerfully.

I realised the door was open and there was a danger staff could hear, so I quickly shut it. "It is. I was there!"

"When you've been married a long time, you have to spice things up. Cynthia goes out, assumes another name, tells me all about it and we have a giggle. At my age and my size, I can't keep her happy that way. You know, she's a great mother and sings in the church choir."

"Of course she does," I said to myself.

"How about we go back to our place over lunch, just the three of us?" suggested Cynthia. "I have a new toy from Lovehoney I want to try."

"That's a wonderful idea, petal. I could make some soup," suggested Keith. "Is mushroom soup okay?"

"I think there's been enough mushrooms ingested here for one day."

I politely left. Never have I been so happy to see the M25 and M1. I arrived home. The painting was done and the rooms in my house were ready to be rented out.

Then the world changed.

Covid-19. Coronavirus. Lockdown. I lost everything. My revenue went to zero as clients put staff on furlough and events were cancelled. How was I supposed to pay the bills? How would I survive with all speaking slots at business conferences gone and all my sales training cancelled?

News distracted me and was on all day. I became addicted to social media, trying to sort my problems out – except nothing was getting sorted.

I asked my father for advice. He told me to order some Indian food, do charity work for a week and God would take care of everything.

Just to be clear, this man went to a top medical university, is a qualified surgeon for which you need to be super-smart, was awarded an MBE from Prince Charles (now King Charles) in 2014, and this was his astute advice – order Indian food, do charity work and God will take care of you.

And that's exactly what I did. I supported charities every day and helped businesses that were struggling every night with their sales, all for free. I promoted them across all my social media channels although it was LinkedIn that made the big difference, since I had an engaged audience of over 5,000 followers at the time and was recently awarded the coveted LinkedIn Top Voice in Sales, given to only ten people in the world.

After two weeks, charities and business owners promoted me on LinkedIn, thanking me for my generosity and telling everyone about me ... and I got sales coaching enquiries. It wasn't much, but enough to pay the bills for a while. Then I did some of the best work of my career in the shortest space of time.

- I finished my second book, *The Easy Guide to Sales for Business Owners*, which outsold all my expectations.

- Launched a sales and wellbeing podcast called "Thrive in Sales".
- Created a high-ticket mastermind group.
- Launched a series of high-ticket sales webinars.
- I reread every business book and sales book in my bookshelf – almost two hours of studying every day, seven days a week.

I lived and breathed my work. By June I was back in profit … although my mental health had taken a battering. There's only so long you can hide in your work. Four months of no hugs, rarely seeing anyone except the people at the Chinese, kebab house and Indian takeaways. The coffee houses and hotels where I met clients and did my writing were shut.

That kind of isolation is unbearable. Some of the sparkle had gone from my eyes. I felt jaded and overweight. I became overwhelmed more easily. Most of all, I was scared of becoming suicidal again. I knew if I took action that somehow it might be okay.

Business Lesson Learned

Things will often happen in life while you are making plans. These will throw you off course and it's tough to get back on track.

Stay focused on the big picture. It will help you through the toughest times. Focus always leads to better thinking. It helps you manage your time and get more good work done.

There's so much distraction in a digital world that will throw you off course. It's easy to spend all day scrolling mindlessly or, worse, trying to multi-task.

One of the world's greatest innovators, Steve Jobs, said "Focus is key for success". Steve knew.

Chapter 9

INVEST IN YOURSELF

One of the joys of having a decent career is that I've met people from all walks of life. One of these wonderful people is Laura, a chatty, opinionated, intelligent scale-up consultant from Devon. She was asking for book recommendations on LinkedIn and I recommended my first book, *Everybody Works in Sales* ☺ She bought it and told everyone how good it was. Then I recommended my second book, *The Easy Guide to Sales for Business Owners,* which she also bought, said was amazing and promoted across social media.

Next thing I knew, I was coaching her Facebook group about generating more sales, and I quickly became friends with Laura and her equally brilliant wife, Louise, a leadership performance and wellbeing coach with a girl-next-door appeal who had just set up her own business.

Laura insisted I was too decent a man to be alone and offered to give me some advice on my dating profile. This is what I sent her:

I enjoy Love Actually, Mamma Mia and The Holiday. I'm a lovely guy who has been hurt. I will never hurt you.

I don't want to say today's music is awful and young people don't know what good music is but today's music is awful and young people don't know what good music is.

I'm not into one-night stands but won't object if you prefer that.

I wasn't going to say my job title was a sales coach. People don't trust people who work in sales, so I said author.

Why did the man cross the road? He heard the chicken was a slut.

Here's a picture of me in a tux. Everybody kept giving me their drinks order. Ha ha.

I won't repeat what Laura said but it sounded like, "What the clucking bell were you thinking writing this rollocks?"

So Laura worked her magic, rewrote the words, took photos of me from my private Facebook page (even though we're not Facebook friends, which means I will never argue with her ever). She made vast improvements on my original version. This is what I had on dating site, Match …

Born and raised in Belfast to Indian parents. Lived in England for thirty years. Proud of all three worlds that I live in and still have my Northern Irish accent (more Liam Neeson than DUP politician).

I love rock 'n' roll from The Beatles to Bon Jovi, relaxing country walks, meditation and doing crazy things like skydiving for cancer charities wearing a blue wig for Willen Hospice, to sporting a handlebar moustache for Movember.

Father of a brilliant daughter who has graduated university.

You don't have to share all my interests. You do have to be kind, honest, enjoy a good laugh and believe in love.

A great variety of pictures accompanied the text. It was

well written, and straight to the point. I even sound interesting. Unlike most men who only say what they think women want to hear, everything on my dating profile was real.

At the same time, I set up an account with eharmony. The snob in me believed in always paying for quality. Match was £20 a month and eharmony was £42 a month, so I figured it would be better. It wasn't. It takes forty-five minutes to go through the questions and profile matching.

Unlike Match, which had a huge variety of women, eharmony had fifty per cent fewer women and most of them had no photos. However, I had to pay six months in advance. That's 6 x £42 = too much money.

Eharmony customer services gave the lazy corporate response that some women take time putting their photos on the site, which is nonsense. You never reply to someone without a photo, and many of these women had none. That's what I dislike most about online dating agencies – certain ones like eharmony take advantage of so many people when they're at their most vulnerable.

So what do you say to someone you don't know online?

"Hi, how are you? How's the weather?" Yup, that's a romance killer. Instead, I looked at their profile, saw what we had in common and talked about that instead.

As a sales coach, I can connect with people quickly and easily. Online dating seemed like a different dimension. I couldn't ask, "What's the biggest challenge facing you right now in business?" or "What deadline are you working to?" or "What happens if you don't get this problem sorted?"

Luckily, I'm well-travelled, so I could talk about their dream destinations. Many had dogs and I enjoy walking my friends' dogs, so that was useful. Some were into personal development so I recommended books by Marie Forleo, Eleanor Roosevelt and Brené Brown. If they liked tennis, my brother is a coach so I discussed Wimbledon. If gin was their cup of tea (so to speak), I recommended gin festivals, since that was my ex-wife's indulgence. I was able to find something in common with most women.

I was honest, easy-going and wanted to show that (unlike many married men who join dating websites for a sexual thrill), that wasn't me. Being genuine and open and accessible was a guaranteed way for women to contact me ...

... but not a single woman replied!

Not one!

I felt that even the drunk women were gazing at my profile and thinking, "God, no, I need a few more drinks before I talk to that bald creature from the abyss."

Because I'd paid extra, I could tell which women were looking at my profile but not making contact. Between fifteen to twenty-five women A DAY were looking at my profile, yet none were getting in touch.

Was that because women like to be contacted first? Was it because they were shy? Was it like shopping, where they could spend several hours looking yet not feel the need to buy anything?

Men aren't like that. In a shop, I know what I want and I'm out within seconds. Even buying stylish business suits takes thirty minutes and I visit two shops in that time.

Maybe the algorithm is such that the dating agencies make you believe women are looking at your profile, so you keep investing time and money with them. After all, if I go incognito on Match (which sounds well dodgy), it costs more money. That means I can see women's profiles without them knowing. If I'm in the spotlight, it means women see my profile before other men and, yes, it costs more money. Everything is designed to make you believe there's a chance of happiness.

In modern dating, that happiness always comes at a price.

Bumble was another disaster. It's a politer version of Tinder, where only women can contact you. You can swipe right if you like a woman and swipe left if you don't. However, the woman contacts you first. I paid Bumble coins to let women know I liked their profile and also paid extra to be in the spotlight. Three hundred pounds later, not one woman had swiped right to show they liked me.

That will destroy your optimism and hope very quickly.

At least I've won £10 here and there on the lottery and scratch cards, yet dating remained elusive.

When I contacted Bumble customer service, they were unhelpful, suggesting I spent more money with them and not reject as many women. I won't settle. I never will. I made that mistake before and it doesn't have a happy ending.

I'm a rational thinker and I need a reason to do things. So if you break up with me, don't ignore me, just give me an explanation.

I had to understand why ninety-nine per cent of women were not replying to me. When you're on a dating website, you can often see who else is online. Ninety-nine per cent of women were NEVER online. How is that possible?

Were these profiles fake? There are plenty of men like me who are desperate for love, connection and the warmth of a body that isn't their own.

What happens when you're desperate? You make bad decisions like giving more money to dating websites.

It's not like newspapers or government say bad things to keep us scared so we live in fear and … wait! Never mind.

So I went back to my sales coaching skills – what happens when nobody replies to my emails or voice mail?

I must follow up.

Hi Ciabatta – (I appreciate many women don't want to use their real name but come on. What's next? Tina Tiger Bread, Sandra Sourdough?)

I liked your profile, messaged you and didn't hear back. I know it's not easy finding the right person. To show you I'm the real deal, here's my LinkedIn profile: https://uk.linkedin.com/in/nkapur and you're welcome to google "Niraj Kapur". There's pages about me, my life, my coaching work, my books and my podcast.

Replies included:

1. I don't think you're right for me.
2. You're too far away (Note: most women want someone local or within thirty miles, which makes it more difficult since there's fewer options. Many of the women matched to me were ninety miles from Milton Keynes, approximately ninety minutes' drive with no traffic. Nobody wants to travel that far for a first or second date).
3. They blocked me.
4. They made racist comments.
5. They tried to charge me for sex.

Why would you block me for following up after a week? I'm

not sending you inappropriate pics, not that I would anyway. In fact, on Match, Bumble and eharmony, you can't send pictures.

You'd think blocking me is the worst thing you could do to someone you've never met or spoken to but racism is worse.

"I want a white man, are you blind?????" screamed Kristina, a rock chick with long dark hair, nose piercing and arm tattoos. One question mark is enough. I hadn't looked at her profile carefully enough. Kristina only wanted Caucasian men, which is common among women in the UK – unfortunately, not all of them state that in their profile.

A good-looking black man is different. Many women secretly dream of that, more than would admit to it publicly. No English woman searches for a short, bald Indian man unless he's rich.

I was tempted to "catfish", where I put up different pictures of a handsome man, just to see the reaction I'd get … but that's not me. I'm not the liar, the bad boy or the bastard. I'm the nice guy. The decent bloke. I'm your friend. That's why I get rejected so much. What if I was the bastard? I can't do that because I don't want to hurt anyone.

As for the prostitutes, there's a LOT of them on dating websites. They're the ones who try to get you off as quickly as possible (no pun intended) and show too much interest in you. A conversation with them goes like this:

Woman: Hey Cutie!
Me: Me?
Woman: Yes you. I like you. You're different to the others.
Me: I know, I have ears like Dumbo.
Woman; You're funny x. Do you like my pics?

Me: Yes, you look nice.
Woman: Would you like to see more?
Me: I'm a guy, of course I would.
Woman: Then click on this link.

And they take you to a website where you have to pay £7.99 to talk with them. Once they take your money, you never hear from them again. Only a fool would do this this more than once. Okay I did it a few times.

Match are good at getting rid of women like this. So far I've seen over thirty women blocked and that's just me!

Tinder was intimidating since everyone was so young compared to me. I kept my profile on there and even put up a shirtless pic from several years ago on the beach when I had a personal trainer and was in good shape. It made no difference. Nobody wanted to contact me. It's a site that works on your looks and no woman was interested in how I looked.

Like Tinder, Plenty of Fish has a reputation for being more about sex and one-night stands than dating. If that's true, I never saw that. I was simply ignored most of the time.

I was getting nowhere with online dating, so decided to invest in a dating coach.

So I type "dating coach" into Google and decide to talk to three experts.

PS: When you type "dating coach" into Google, you get 197,000,000 results.

When you want to lose weight, you go online for advice. The disadvantage of this approach is that you're inundated with an overwhelming number of recommendations and conflicting advice.

Some will advise you to eat cheese and butter, others say avoid dairy at all costs.

Some will advise you to eat meat and veg with no carbs, yet others will insist carbs are a vital part of dieting.

Some will insist you need to lift weights to lose body weight, others insist on long-distance running instead.

Marni Kinrys, known as "Your Wing Girl" comes across as an in-your-face American. She's actually from Canada. She tells it like it is and looks stunning on camera. Marni sits on her bed, her eyes drawing you in, touching her beautiful brunette hair and moving her svelte body with ease. She has 919,000 subscribers on her YouTube channel. Titles include:

- Saying THIS attracts all women
- How to make a woman be attracted to you instantly
- Why women are attracted to jerks

Kate Spring is a men's dating and attraction coach, who often appears in what looks like a nightdress. She also looks stunning on camera, yet her personality is hard to read. She has 171,000 subscribers on her YouTube channel. I signed up to her email newsletter since she sells herself effortlessly – and being a sales coach I admire that.

I received an email every day, a very American style which annoys British people. Some of the emails had value, sometimes I got sold to badly – one message lasted *thirty minutes!* I had to unsubscribe, it was too much to read things like:

7 Innocent Words That Make Any Girl Chase You
Warning: This video will come down soon so watch until the very end

The email below was overly sexual, yet I can see how it would appeal to many men. Women like Kate could sell men anything and we would buy it because we're visual creatures. Examples of what she spoke about included:

Use this trick to sleep around or use it to get a girlfriend that's out of your league.
The choice is yours.
But you have to act fast because it's only online until …

Our friends on the other side of the Atlantic really know how to sell by creating urgency.

Bobby Rio has 257,000 YouTube subscribers and claims to have 213,000 newsletter subscribers. He's written books like *Make Her Beg You to Bang Her* (10 out of 10 for subtlety), *Unlock Her Legs* (I'm actually embarrassed to type out these sexist titles) and *Make Small Talk Sexy* plus he has hundreds of YouTube videos. He's got short brown hair and is the kind of nameless, faceless man you could meet in any office. His videos are slick and well spoken.

None of these coaches come across with any warmth, yet they all give practical advice. Maybe that's how the dating world works.

What's interesting is that all these gurus are advising men!

Their advice made sense when you met a woman in a bar. But here's the nub of the problem.

People over forty are less likely to meet their future partner in a bar. Plus, social distancing and lockdown make online dating the best option.

Dating gurus are similar to financial gurus: they talk good theory, but not enough practical advice.

Financial gurus tell you that eighty per cent of money is in the mind. Well, it must be in the mind because it's not in my bank account! You can think as positively as you like – but without business acumen, networking abilities, experience, opportunities, a workaholic nature, a willingness to sacrifice family time, and a little luck, you are not going to get rich.

I read an article by Kate Spring: *How to Get a Girlfriend.* Again, loads of good advice, such as how you need to be in control of yourself, yet she said it's important to have female friends, because if there are other women around you, single women will be intrigued.

All my friends are women, so I can confirm that this advice doesn't work for me.

My ex-wife Priyanka was stunning and her glamorous friends were hot. When I'd walk into a restaurant, coffee shop or party, men would stare. Some women would give them dirty looks, other would admire them, yet no woman ever asked me out as a result. Comments would vary from, "Your wife is pretty" to "How did you get a wife like that?"

Men simply called me a "jammy bastard".

So I decided to find a British dating coach, figuring she would not try to upsell me to her courses. As a coach myself, I understand that people want to learn new things from me and get results. I project a sense of warmth and show that I really care.

You know the old saying often attributed to Abraham Lincoln: "People don't care how much you know until they know how much you care."

The dating coaches I found through mutual friends in my network gave me a free introductory session each, which I was grateful for, but I didn't get a feeling that they listened. I felt that they just wanted to sell me their coaching programmes, which they all failed to do.

Finally, I found Hayley Quinn on Google. She has 2.7m views of her Ted Talk and is a dating coach recommended by Match. She was less in-your-face, had depth and warmth and guess what? She was stunningly beautiful. A model with a warm personality. What I liked most though, was that her advice wasn't just for men, it was for women too, and that made me feel at ease.

She didn't talk about how to meet someone in a bar, but how you talk to them online.

If someone doesn't have anything on their profile, ask them this: "Tell me something I wouldn't know from your profile."

If they go on lots of holidays, tell them, "I don't know about you, but I've booked my va-cays until 2021."

A lot of the advice she gives is similar to my coaching – it's okay to pause and have silence. You don't have to keep talking. Listening is vital. I always practise what I teach so I followed through on this.

Never say, "Hi, how are you doing in lockdown?" Oops. I've said that to everyone!

The best part was, when you want to kiss a woman, don't just lean in. Ask, "So, are we going to kiss?" or "Can I be a bit cheeky and kiss you?" I like that, it's asking permission.

Being a coach myself, I'm a huge believer in investing in coaching. I was so close to doing that when I attended a live training session with Hayley Quinn.

For ninety minutes she owned the screen, thanks to her charisma, beauty and intelligence. Hayley wasn't just giving advice. She IS the woman most men aspire to be with. Her advice was better than any dating coach, yet there was still so much that didn't make sense.

- ✓ Pay attention to your profile – agreed and already done.
- ✓ Complete your profile in full – agreed and already done.
- ✓ Don't have only one or two photos, that's too few. Have three to six – agreed and already done.
- ✓ I'm the kind of person that would give you my last Rolo – I love this idea and have implemented it on my profile. It made no difference and nobody ever refers to it.
- ✓ Avoid clichés like "If my friends had to describe me they would say xxxx" or "I'm looking for a partner-in-crime."
- ✓ Don't ask, "How long have you been single?" or "How long have you been on Match?" My bad, I always ask that.
- ✓ Don't ask somebody out in the first message – I never do.

- × If they say they like a particular movie genre like horror, ask for a recommendation – this doesn't work, I've tried it many times. Maybe they associate me with Freddy Krueger or Jason from *Halloween*.
- × Have fun and be curious – this doesn't work, I've tried it many times.
- × For your dating profile, make sure you're looking directly at the camera – this doesn't work, I've tried it many times.
- × Have different outfits on in your photos so it doesn't look like you've taken them all on the same day – this doesn't work, I've tried it many times.

I'm implementing this without cynicism, yet the results always make me cynical. So I watched over 100 YouTube videos and took notes. My best takeaways from everything I learned online were:

a) Don't agree with everything a woman says. Too many guys do that. Have your own opinion – I agree.
b) How you dress matters – I agree.
c) Make eye contact – I agree.
d) Be fun to be around – I agree.
e) Be in good shape – I had put on four stones since my divorce and none of my clothes fitted me anymore. I don't do drugs, smoke or drink. Junk food, chocolate, cake and carbs are my only comfort in life. The older you get, the more brutal it is to lose weight – I agree that I needed to lose weight.
f) Smile – when I smile, I look like a vampire due to my corner teeth having fangs. As a result, I don't show my teeth in photos and many people think I have no teeth – I agree.
g) Be a bastard but don't be a jerk. Confused? Yes, me too.
h) Don't reply to a woman when she texts you. Make her wait and think you're busy – I'll agree to disagree.
i) When you're with a woman, touch her arm or back for a moment. She's more likely to be attracted to you – I've tried that before and it works.
j) When she talks to you, listen. Don't look at other women – I made that mistake during my marriage.
k) When a woman talks to you, don't forget her name – I made that mistake during my marriage.

l) When she makes an effort to look good, compliment her. Don't say, "Is that what you're wearing?" I made that mistake during … you get the point.

Every second I wondered who I would meet. What would they be like? Would they have suffered loneliness and mental health problems like me or would they be normal? There's someone out there for everyone, I have to believe that. I need to believe that. Waking up in the morning, I was consumed with a yearning that my life would be complete only if I had a partner.

Dating is addictive. Like when you first get Facebook and you're on the app every ten minutes to see who has liked you and commented on your post. You get endorphin highs. It goes back to the fact that as human beings, we want attention. We want recognition. It's why social media has taken over the world. We are addicted to the thrill of a like. Unlike hard drugs, alcohol and fatty foods where you can see the damage and get help, you can't see the long-term damage social media does to our brains. Online dating is no different. A ping at 2.30 a.m. I would jump out of bed and gaze at the phone with my groggy eyes, to see who had liked my profile.

Usually, it was a woman with no picture, which is always a strict no. If someone doesn't show their profile pic, what are they hiding? Answer: it's not shyness.

When I go to bed at night, my phone is in my hand as I look at the profiles of women I would be with. The beautiful sea of white. I rarely saw any women of colour on these platforms. Out of 100 women I viewed every day, three were black, one was Asian and one was Indian. Growing up in Northern Ireland, I was surrounded by white girls, that was what I wanted. When I worked in London, despite the amazing richness of culture and people, in sales, it was white women who I worked with. That was who I saw, mixed with, talked to, met at the crappy coffee machines before anyone knew what good coffee was.

So I tried to find some balance in my life. Charity work had become important to me later in life. My only regret is that I didn't discover it sooner. One of the best ways to get your mind off yourself is to help other people.

Local charities make up the bulk of charities in the UK. It's always best to help locally. They have lower overheads, no CEOs getting six-figure salaries with extortionate bonuses.

I get no kicks from standing outside a supermarket with a bucket and collecting loose change. I want to make a more significant difference.

After a fortnight of charity work and giving back to the world, from free sales and marketing advice to free LinkedIn training to free advice on fundraising events, my confidence had grown again and life had more meaning. I genuinely believe that what you give to the world will come back to you.

After a break from dating and giving everything I could to help others, I turned on my computer at home …

… and the goodwill came back to me. I may have mentioned I'm not crazy about eharmony, yet suddenly women were messaging me from there. It wasn't movie-star status, more like "thanks for your message, I liked your profile".

Within a few exchanges, I had dates set up. It happened very quickly. That suited me fine. Who has time to waste talking online all the time?

It was my first date in twenty-two years as a single man and I had no idea what I was in for.

Business Lesson Learned

Invest in yourself. It's the smartest thing you can do. The more you learn, the more you earn. Often, you get so stuck inside your world that you need clarity. That's where a coach comes in.

All the best athletes have coaches; fitness, nutrition, mindset. Same with the top movie stars and singers. The most successful people have speaking coaches, health coaches or business coaches to advise them.

You need a coach to help you see things differently, keep you accountable, push you and take you to another level.

If you don't invest in yourself, why would anyone invest in you?

Chapter 10

PHYSICAL HEALTH

My first date was with Hermione. When I told my female friends, they were excited and wished me good luck. When I told my male friends, they all had the same dumb response: "Hermione from Harry Potter?"

According to her profile, Hermione worked as a nurse in London. She was mother to three kids, she had a friendly smile, was in her early forties, looking for a "nice" man and enjoyed coffee, cake and gardening. She wasn't attractive nor was she ugly. Referring to someone as average sounds unflattering and I don't make notes rating women out of ten.

English summers can be rainy and miserable. When it's sunny it can be glorious, suddenly the whole world makes sense. But in Britain we sometimes get a heatwave and the date took place on one of those sticky days.

It was over thirty degrees. Humid, intense heat where the air is stale. Despite our desire for more heat in the country, you actually crave a breeze or air-con or stronger deodorant when it gets that bad.

How can you wear a smart shirt and trousers on a day like that? Instead, I wore my shorts to show off my sprinter's legs. The denim shorts made my thighs look strong. My calves were tough and the back of my calves were accentuated when I walked. Priyanka used to say there were two things she liked about my body: my legs and … well, I'm not going to mention the other part.

Hermione and I met in a car park, which sounds weird but it wasn't. It was an easy meeting spot and that's the story I'm sticking to. Thankfully, Hermione looked just like her photo. I gave her a warm bear hug. She gave me a half-hearted hug back. Some people find hugging weird. I don't, it's my way of showing affection.

"What's the smell?" she asked.

"Marks and Spencer's aftershave or body odour," I proudly replied.

"M & S?" she replied, sarcastically. "Classy."

"It's Dermot O'Leary, the bloke from that reality show. Smells lovely and it's cheap. Cashback." Don't know why I said "cashback". Never used it in a sentence in my life, before today.

I took her to the Sunday market, which was shut due to lockdown. Then I took her to my favourite coffee shop, which was shut due to a lack of staff caused by lockdown. We ended up at the garden centre.

Hermione was in her element. She kept pointing to flowers, the names of which I couldn't pronounce. We had crispy fish and chips and mushy peas for lunch, then bought overpriced posh farmers' fruit and veg to take home.

We were so comfortable around each other. I expected awkwardness, long silences and complaining about exes. The one-hour lunch lasted three hours. I offered to drive her back to the car park, but she insisted on us spending more time together. I touched her arm and lower part of her back many times. She didn't object.

I asked myself, *could I introduce Hermione to my family and friends*? The answer was a resounding YES.

I dropped her back at the car park and gave her a surprise from the boot of my car: I'd stopped at a cherry orchard on the way over and picked up a punnet of freshly picked cherries. She tried one and 'ummed' with delight. Supermarket cherries don't compare.

Moving in closer, I took Hayley Quinn's fantastic advice and said, "So, are we going to kiss?"

Hermione squirmed. "Sorry, you're … not my type. Can we be friends?"

"No. No, we can't. Why did you spend this much time with me if you weren't interested? I've wasted my entire Sunday afternoon!"

That's what I should have said. Instead I was terribly British and polite. I apologised for being ugly.

I felt horrible. All she had to say was "It's not you, it's me" to completely insult me.

"It's not you, it's me," she then replied. Before awkwardly going back to her car. She opened the driver's door, turned around, mouthed "I'm sorry" and drove away.

I sat in my car. The leather seats burned my bare legs from the heat. I stared hard in the rear-view mirror: my large nose, double chin and brown skin stared back at me. It's a look I can't escape and I hate it. Sweat dripped from my forehead then trickled down the sides. Shadows covered my face. I looked like Marlon Brando in *Apocalypse Now*, slowly being drawn into insanity.

There was no doubt about it. No matter what women say about wanting a "nice" man, what they actually want is an attractive man or someone who is bad for them. I decided I would do everything I could to eat better, get into shape and become God's gift to women.

I drove to the nearest gym to become a member. Before osteoarthritis wrecked my right knee, I was a gym bunny. You know those men who work out in front of the mirror, admiring their fantastic bodies and trying to impress all the attractive women? Unfortunately, that was me.

The gym macho men focus mainly on the upper torso; the powerful chest from inclined push-ups and dumbbell curls, bulging biceps they can show off in T-shirts from dumbbell curls, ripped triceps from dips and more dumbbell curls.

Your shoulders give you the bouncer look with dumbbell lifts and working your back in conjunction with the pull-downs. Your stomach gets a six-pack with protein drinks, no sugar, protein food, no fruit because that contains sugar, and 100 sit-ups a day.

Within six months, you're in shape and, within a year, you have a beach body.

Some gym macho men would oil themselves up and take pics. Some would lie on cheap sunbeds to get a tan. I already have an amazing tan so that didn't appeal to me.

Most Indian men my age are out of shape from a diet of potatoes, bread and rice every night, plus a massive yearning for anything sweet. That's part of the three things all Indian men crave. Sweet food, money and white women. We have little luck with English women, so we overindulge in the first two. Why do you think we drive Mercedes, BMWs and Range Rovers. No Indian man drives a Smart car or an electric Nissan Leaf.

The first gym was shut due to lockdown. The second gym was shut due to lockdown. Nothing was open. How could I work out and get in shape with gyms and swimming pools shut? Cycling bores me to tears despite Milton Keynes having some of the best cycling paths in the UK. Contrary to popular belief, long-distance running isn't ideal. It helps you lose weight, but you don't get into a killer shape for the ladies.

My female clients keep telling me about this guy called Joe Wicks who does workouts on YouTube. I can see why they talk about him around the virtual water cooler.

I got changed into my T-shirt and shorty shorts. Started jogging on the spot to warm up. Ah, my right knee hurts. Damn osteoarthritis.

Then I squat down and lift my arms up. That hurts my knee again and twinges my torn rotator cuff in my right shoulder, an injury caused by incompetent GPs who care more about seeing as many patients as possible – more patients, more cash – than treating my shoulder properly. My father is always quick to defend the NHS in England, saying how they're overrun and the shoulder is a complicated body part. When several GPs, several shoulder experts/consultants and several physios all screw up, something is seriously wrong with the NHS; I don't care if it's free.

Next up, get on your back, hands against your head, twist your body, elbows to knees. The intense summer heat means my T-shirt is stuck to my back, which is stuck to the floor. I open the back doors and windows for fresh air. It makes no difference.

I plug in a fan which spends eleven months and three weeks of the year in the garage and I get into a coughing fit when all the gathered dust sprays in every direction.

I take a few paracetamol to numb the pain from my shoulder and knee. I have to get into shape for dating. Push-ups next. I do one push-up, my rotator cuff gives way and I slam my jaw on the floor.

Four hours later, I woke up on the sofa feeling groggy. I had consumed an entire tub of Ben & Jerry's Phish Food ice-cream: a delightful combination of corn syrup, butter, sugar, milk and several other ingredients that are definitely not good for you.

Nobody likes to be rejected. In business it hurts too, yet I always find the strength to get back on my feet and fight. In my personal life, it hit me harder. I struggled up from the sofa and asked my coaching clients for help. Surely they must know a single woman they could set me up with?

I'm different compared to most coaches since most of my clients are women.

There are a lot of female coaches warning women to "avoid men" because "men are aggressive". While there are some horrendous male coaches out there in the business world, most of the ones I've met are fairly decent and only want the best for their clients.

Because I lead with kindness and openness, women read my posts on LinkedIn. They bought my first book *Everybody Works in Sales.* I openly discussed my feelings. When I set goals, they weren't just business goals, I would ask about a client's personal goals. I discussed overcoming failure, making mistakes, battling depression and the challenges that come with being a working parent.

Women connected with this. So naturally, after every coaching session, I asked my clients if any of their girlfriends, sisters or mothers were single.

Wendy was one of my middle-aged clients who ran a successful logistics business. She inherited the business from her father, doubled the size and tripled the profits. She had become overwhelmed with work and increased competition, so I helped improve her mindset and time management. I taught her how to sell better in a competitive environment. As a thank you, she introduced me to her friend, Yasmin, who she told me "had issues".

"I appreciate that, Wendy, but I have no interest in dating a woman with issues."

"You want to meet a woman in her forties who's normal? Good luck with that," retorted Wendy.

"What kind of issues?" I asked, reluctantly. "Drugs, drink, pyromania?"

"That's a good start," she replied.

"A good start?" I explained. "I can't date someone more screwed up than me, it's asking for trouble."

"People are complicated," explained Wendy. "I have another meeting, hon. Good luck, and not to make you worry, but keep your wallet on you at all times."

"Say what?"

Wendy had hung up. I called my other clients, hoping for more options. They informed me their friends were all in relationships, or, in a few cases, not my type.

Dazed and confused, I wore my Iron Maiden T-shirt, denim jacket, Dr Martens boots and jeans. We arrived at her restaurant of choice: Paris House, a Michelin-starred restaurant in a wealthy Buckinghamshire village, inhabited by the landed gentry and wealthy Londoners who enjoyed having a second home in the country.

Unfortunately, I hadn't researched the restaurant Yasmin had picked. Everyone judged me as I walked in. Yasmin wore a designer dress. She was in her late forties but looked several years younger. The glow of her skin showed she took care of herself. Her diamond earrings twinkled, which showed she liked the good life. An expensive-looking bottle of champagne was on ice. She was enjoying a sip.

"Hi, it's Niraj. How are you?"

Yasmin immediately put a menu over her face to avoid me. I moved in closer. She hid further under the menu. It had skate, suckling pig and an exquisite tasting menu on display. I was more interested in dessert: banana split – not had one of those since I was a kid.

"Hi, Yasmin?"

She slowly peeked over the menu. "Hello, um, nice outfit."

"Yeah, listen, I didn't dress for the occasion. Do you fancy a KFC?" I suggested. "Burger, chips, gravy and corn on the cob. A winning combo."

She stared at me like I had run over her cat.

"I'm not poor, although my surname is Kapur," I said, cracking up laughing. Nobody else joined in.

"Wendy is always setting me up," said Yasmin. "Bless her, she's a good friend and means well, but you're not what I was expecting …"

"Didn't she send a photo?" I asked.

"She said you were Irish and not in prison. That's good enough for me."

"So, what's the problem?"

Question asked and answered.

An awkward pause followed, which seemed to last forever. When women hear I'm Irish, they assume I'm white and are surprised by my skin colour. My whole life I've wished I was white. It would have caused less judgement, fewer problems and a lot less heartache. The further outside London you travel (apart from the big cities), the more women assume Irish = white. It's what they grew up with and what they prefer. It would be wonderful to think we live in a world where your personality is more important than skin colour, but we don't.

"You're not the Irish I was expecting."

That offended me. "What were you expecting? A man wearing green saying, 'top of the morning, would you like a potato?' A man carrying a barrel of Guinness? Bono?"

My voice sounded louder than I meant it to.

"It's not that, you're a just a bit …" She didn't say the word, but she did inflate her cheeks for a second.

I sat down. "Let's not ruin the evening," I said. "Close your eyes and imagine I'm thin. After five minutes, if you're not interested, we can leave."

"You mean I can leave?" she asked, confused.

"Yes, sorry. You can leave. I'm a bit out of practice."

"Sounds like a plan. Why don't you get yourself a drink? I need the ladies."

Yasmin stood up from the table. I stood up as well – a great habit my father had taught me as a sign of respect to women.

I ordered a Diet Coke for myself and poured champagne from Yasmin's bottle into her glass. Ten minutes later, there was no sign of her. A moment later, while gazing out the window to avoid the looks from judgemental diners, I saw her rush outside and get into a taxi.

This was so humiliating. That was two horrible experiences in two days because of my looks. I didn't think it could get any worse. How wrong I was. I asked for the waiter for the bill. It came to £113.

My Diet Coke was £3. The bottle of champagne was £110.

I would never look at another woman again. All they ever did was reject me and make me feel bad about myself.

My phone pinged. It was Sarah from eharmony. She wanted to meet.

Depression over. Men are such fickle creatures and so easily pleased.

Business Lesson Learned

Take care of your physical health. It's ideal to think we live in a world where people will like us because we're good people. Sadly, that's not always the case. If you look out of shape, tired or unwell, people will judge. Make the effort to look good. I wish I had; the result would have been much better.

Staying in good health gives you more energy and allows you to perform better at work. It enables you to give better attention to people. It helps with body posture.

When you're healthier, you enjoy work more and often achieve more.

While the gym is ideal, HIIT exercises on YouTube are free. Long walks are free.

It's easy to say you're "too busy". If something is important to you, you will get it done.

Chapter 11

TRUST YOUR GUT

Freya finished her second-year university exams. What an unusual experience it must be to go to university then be forced to spend months in your bedroom doing exams online, unable to see fellow students or socialise on campus due to Covid.

Freya had set off to Australia earlier in the year for her five-month student exchange programme with Monash University in Melbourne. She was the only family I had in England.

Let me rephrase that – she was the only family I wanted to spend time with in England.

When Freya had first gone to university, I'd already mentioned the difficulty of missing her and how it impacted my marriage to Priyanka. At least Freya returned home every fortnight to get her clothes washed or ask for money.

Australia was a different story. Five months without my baby. Yes, I know she's nineteen, but she'll always be my baby: no asking me to pick her up at 3 a.m. from a nightclub, no seeing her in public with her friends and her pretending she hadn't seen me, no rolling her eyes at me when I asked if I was a cool dad.

PS: No dad looks cool in front of his teenage daughter. The harder you try, the worse you appear.

Seven weeks after Freya left for university in Australia, Covid hit the UK badly. Freya's course had already been delayed because the Chinese and South Korean students were in quarantine. Freya went travelling around Sydney and Melbourne and had a blast; those cities were thankfully not affected at the beginning of the worldwide pandemic. Warwick University, where Freya was studying global sustainable development, flew everyone back to the UK from Australia after seven weeks.

Freya, being independent, said she had spent thousands of pounds flying to the other side of the earth, why not travel? When would she get this opportunity again and, my favourite one, if you loved me you'd let me travel. I called Priyanka, who only now speaks to me regarding our daughter, and we both agreed on an extra week of holiday and the flight back home … a week later, there were no flights back to England from Sydney.

That was worrying. Freya flew to Japan in gloves and a mask, had to wait several hours, then flew from Tokyo to London.

When she arrived at Heathrow, Priyanka was there. Even in ripped jeans and white trainers, her hair tied back and making little effort, she was gorgeous. Priyanka said a brief hello like it was a random colleague at work, then went back to whatever she was doing on her phone. Tension was still there between us. Maybe it was my vulnerability, but I still had feelings for Priyanka. I always will. The fact I can never have her and that quite a few men glanced over at her presence heightened everything.

Twenty-one years is a long time to be married. We had lots of problems, but we also had some good times …

Our Christmas holiday to Prague in the freezing cold, visiting the stunning castle and drinking hot chocolate at the market. The warmth and wonder of Kalkan in Turkey while staying at a villa with a swimming pool and having a chef making a smorgasbord of fresh, intoxicating food every day. Doing a boudoir video shoot for my birthday; just to be clear, I wasn't doing the boudoir shoot, that would be a punishment. My limited edition TAG Heuer Carrera watch for my fortieth. Making our house a beautiful home. Priyanka had done so much to make my life happy.

Now she was ignoring me like most women did on dating websites. I wished she knew how much I still cared about her and how sorry I was for not being attentive enough as a husband.

Freya arrived through Heathrow Airport customs with her suitcases, looking like she was in a sci-fi movie in her gloves and mask. She couldn't hug me. She had to go into quarantine for two weeks since Covid-19 was now a problem worldwide.

"After quarantine, spend three days with me and four days with your mum," I suggested to Freya. "You can have your own space. I won't bother you. You can invite whoever you want around unless it's a boy, in which case I have to meet him first. Sound good?"

"Mum's an amazing cook and I can wear her clothes, so I'm staying with her."

And that was that.

I see Freya every Sunday afternoon. We go for a walk. During the week, she never calls or asks me how I'm doing. She never even texts me to see how I'm coping living on my own and battling mental health. Like her mother, she sees vulnerability as a sign of weakness.

I feel like a prisoner being let out for good behaviour. One of the worst elements of divorce is the effect it can have on your children. Freya loved her mum and Priyanka was a great mum, so they're close to each other. They go shopping, they cook dinner together, they watch awful reality shows and have a wonderful banter with Priyanka's family in India. It still hurts only seeing her once a week for fifteen to twenty minutes. How can you create any kind of bond?

With nothing else going on in my life, I had Sarah to focus on. Everything about Sarah was perfect; she likes me when she's sober. She has a great sense of humour. I find her attractive. She lives five minutes' drive from my house.

I washed my car inside and out until it sparkled and hung a pine air freshener from my rear-view mirror. I arrived at Sarah's place and had a shock. It was in a rough part of town: abandoned council flats, a mattress lying on the ground and rubbish overflowing from bins.

She exited her flat without a care, greeting me with an enthusiastic hug. I opened the car door for her, took one last look around, trying not to be judgemental, and drove to Out of Office – they do amazing fry-ups, which are not easy to find in Milton Keynes.

As we arrived, I opened the car door again. "You're such a gentleman," cooed Sarah as she kissed me on the cheek. It lasted a good second. Sensations ran up and down my body. Then she whispered in my ear, "You look good."

That's all I wanted. For someone to recognise me and make me feel special and Sarah had aced it.

"I want our picture all over social media," she insisted. "And tag me in."

I took out my phone and we had a selfie. We looked like a couple in love. Even when we ordered breakfast from the waiter, we never took our eyes off each other.

Sarah talked about being separated from her husband and kids. I could tell it was causing her pain, yet she remained tough.

"Wasn't that difficult?" I asked.

"My husband is a control freak. Couldn't wait to get out of there."

"I get that but …" I didn't want to ask.

"What?"

"Leaving your kids. How was that?"

"They're teenagers, I couldn't wait to leave them. Annoying fuckers."

It was a warning sign. I should have paid attention, but I dismissed it.

"You and your husband …?"

"It's over. The flat was all I could afford on my salary."

Sarah stacked shelves in Sainsbury's. It didn't pay much, then again she wasn't materialistic She didn't own a car and her husband had always paid the bills, so she worked for her kids and for booze, like any decent mother. There was no desire in her to earn loads, just enough to get by. It was nice to meet someone who was content doing that.

"Show me your phone," Sarah asked.

"Are you going to send inappropriate pictures of yourself to my wife?" I replied.

"Of course not," she said, innocently.

"Then I'm definitely not giving you my phone," I replied.

She seductively took my fingers, interlocking them with

hers. Her nails skimmed over my skin. A tingle spread all over me. Excitement and horniness.

Sarah took my forefinger, then at lightning speed, put it on my iPhone causing it to unlock. She giggled and snatched my phone. I rushed to her side to take it back from her. She wouldn't relinquish it, so I tickled her. She shrieked with pure joy as we wrestled over the phone.

"Let's go back to your place and screw each other's brains out," she suggested.

"Yes, oh, God. Yes, Lord Jesus. Thank you. I DESERVE THIS!" I almost shouted.

At home, we rushed inside. Not only did I not lock the door, but I didn't close it. My neighbours could have stolen what they wanted, it was all second-hand.

It was the first time in a year I had been intimate with anyone. This meant so much to me. It wasn't a drunken one-night stand. This was passion and hope and a much-needed release.

The stairs were draped with our discarded clothes.

In my bedroom, I closed the curtains while Sarah checked herself in the mirror in her bland underwear and bra.

"Wow. You look almost as beautiful as me," I said. Sarah burst out laughing.

Sex shouldn't be too serious. You need to have a good laugh in the process.

"Why don't you let your body do the talking?" suggested Sarah as she ripped my underwear off.

"Hello sailor!" Don't know why I said that.

There was no tenderness, no soft kissing and foreplay, this

was animalistic. Fighting to kiss each other, tongues, moaning … it was heaven.

If you want to read about something raunchy, naughty, powerful and orgasmic, you won't read it here. Certain things I keep private.

I do remember I had no condoms at home. Luckily, before the trip, I'd gone to the local corner shop. I'd had my mask on, the Indian woman behind the glass had her mask on and there was glass in between us, so it was hard to communicate.

There were people queuing behind me. It was 8.30 a.m.

"Do you have any condoms?" I asked, self-consciously.

"We don't have coconuts," said the Indian woman.

"Condoms … Johnnies," I explained. She didn't understand, so I raised my voice. "Johnnies?"

"No Johnny works here," she replied.

I noticed the condoms on the shelf next to the Ibuprofen and Elastoplast.

"Those!" I pointed.

"Ah, condoms," she said, grabbing three packets.

During marriage I'd never worn condoms so had no idea what to buy. Bilyana always had her own forty-eight-condom box set, treating it like a sweet dispenser.

The blue box said *extra safe*. Red said *thin feel* and the yellow and pink said *pleasure me*. I had no idea what gave women sexual thrills. There was a middle-aged woman behind me, but I was too British to ask her opinion.

"Do you maybe have any gin and tonic flavoured ones?" I asked the shopkeeper.

The bell rang as another person entered the shop. The queue was getting longer.

"What would a man like me normally go for?" I asked, desperately.

"Sanjay, do we have extra small condoms?" she called out to a man stacking toilet rolls.

I heard sniggering behind me.

He then called out to Ranjeet in the back, speaking what appeared to be fast South Indian, but managing to work the phrase "small condoms" into the conversation.

To avoid further embarrassment, I paid for all three packets and scooted out of there.

"Let me go on top," Sarah said. She expertly swung me around, took control and ground her hips. It was like she had a motor attached: one minute, two minutes, sweat dripping, her face contorting with pleasure. She cried out so loud, the whole neighbourhood must have heard. I didn't have a problem with that.

Sarah lay down on me and it turned to romance. Soft sweet kisses and cuddles. I could feel her breath on my face and it was heavenly. Nothing else in the world existed.

It had been seven months since I had slept with a woman. It felt like seven years. I wanted to get on my knees and thank God for this divine intervention.

We jumped in the shower to clean up and spooned. To be clear, we didn't spoon in the shower, we dried ourselves with one towel, spooned on my bed and lay there in bliss – my first time making love in a new house and it was perfect. No skeletons in her closet. No rush to leave. No text messages pinging.

Nothing perfect lasts forever, of course and, sure enough, it was about to come crashing down.

Sarah and I binge-watched Netflix, had healthy green

smoothies then walked to the top of Campbell Park where we indulged ourselves in the views. We held hands, even when I was driving, my fingers discovering parts of her fingers and hands I hadn't touched before.

Sarah kept staring into me like she wanted to say, "I love you." I sensed this because that was exactly how I felt. How could I feel so intense about someone I had just met?

We went back home and Sarah activated the video on her mobile and pressed record. I should have questioned this and later regretted not having the strength to say that was not acceptable. When there are warning signs, you need to question them.

"Say my name …" she asked in an exotic voice.

I did. Again and again and again.

I don't know how long she recorded us making love. All I remembered was feeling blissful. There's nothing quite so exciting as a new romance.

The next evening, we had dinner planned at Melis, a fabulous restaurant with a monstrous menu of every delicious local Turkish dish you can imagine. Nine Turkish restaurants have opened up within a ten-mile radius of my house. Every single one served delightful food, bursting with flavour and soul.

Sarah was with her kids and said she would meet me at Melis at 7 p.m. It was one of the hottest nights of the year, yet I strutted inside like I owned the restaurant – which was ironic since a diner thought I was Turkish and asked me what I would recommend for her from the menu. "Iya recommend everything," I replied in an accent that was more exaggerated Italian.

The restaurant was packed with families, kids, friends and couples. I sat by the window as usual. The Turkish waiter brought a basket of warm fresh bread which I dipped in olive oil. Fresh bread from the oven, you make the world a better place, especially when the crust has a crunchiness to it.

That tasted so good, almost illegally good. So I had another slice of bread, dipping it in the aromatic oil, enjoying every morsel and flavour and trying not to scoff it down.

At 7.15 p.m. I called Sarah but there was no answer. I texted. Nothing. She wasn't on social media. For some, that's a red flag. When I deliver sales coaching in offices, I always arrive half an hour earlier to observe office culture. Do people say good morning? Do they support each other? Are they miserable? The thing I notice most is that not only do people often walk into an office with a phone in their hand and check it before work but during their day at work, they glance at their phone *every seven minutes* to check WhatsApp, text messages, social media or dating apps.

In an eight-hour workday, mixed phone distraction with unnecessary meetings and emails pinging, you get three to four hours' work done in eight hours.

With Sarah, it was great to meet someone not obsessed with technology.

Then my stomach turned. You know that feeling you get when something isn't right? You can't quite explain it. It's not indigestion or bloating, yet you know bad news awaits. I sensed danger. I just didn't know what it was.

That video Sarah took last night of us making love, why hadn't she shared it with me? Is that what lovers do in the modern dating scene to tease each other? Would she use it as revenge porn to humiliate me in public?

People were staring at me since I was the only one sitting

alone. We live in a world where people are quick to judge and slow to understand.

The waiter noticed my restlessness and brought more warm bread since I had emptied the first breadbasket. He smiled and asked if I wanted a drink. I explained awkwardly I was waiting for someone.

"I hope your boyfriend arrives soon," said the waiter politely before leaving.

I've been mistaken for being gay on many occasions. I take this as a compliment since every gay man I know is stylish and intelligent. I dress well, I'm kind, adore my mother, and Cher, love the theatre, have a lot of drama in my life and enjoy the good things in life, so it's understandable why this happens.

Ten minutes later, I had dipped all the bread in olive oil and was now stuffed.

At 7.30 p.m., I made another call to Sarah. No answer. A droplet of water stained the tablecloths. It was from my forehead. I dried it with the napkin. My shirt was now sticking to me like I was actually in Turkey in the summer heat.

At 7.45 p.m. Sarah finally picked up.

"Are you okay?" I asked, worried.

There was a long pause.

"Sarah, what's wrong?" I was so concerned something had happened to her.

"I'm back with my ex." There was no emotion in her voice.

If I had been skewered with a kebab, it would have hurt less. I grabbed the napkin and wiped away more sweat, my head pounding.

"Didn't know he was in the picture ..." I said, controlling the urge to vent.

"I wanted to make him jealous," she said, not a hint of remorse in her voice.

"And you used me with that video …" That made sense. "Don't you feel anything for me?"

"We had great sex. Someone who looks like you should be grateful for anything he gets," she said and hung up.

No wonder she had sex with me so quickly. No normal, sober woman does that. It takes time to talk about things that shame you. A week later, I told my female friends and they were wonderful, sympathising and reminding me that I deserved better. My male friends told me I was a "lucky bastard. Boo hoo! A sexy woman shagged you and doesn't want to drag you around the shops. You won't have to listen to stories of her boring family."

My male friends plainly had issues ... and now so did I.

It was the story of my life. No matter how hard I tried, I couldn't quite make it. Like the millions of musicians around the world who never got their lucky break. Like the person who almost made it, then gave up on life to become a shadow of their former self. Like the failed sportsmen who became PE teachers. The world is full of people who failed to reach their full potential. My greatest fear is that I would become one of them.

There are too many middle-aged men in pubs complaining about the government and the state of the world. Even worse, they offer no positive solutions. I didn't want to be one of those clichés. I couldn't let my life go further downhill. There was nowhere else to fall.

The summer heat upstairs was brutal. The carpeted floors in my house didn't help. I opened windows and put the fan on, yet I couldn't stop sweating.

I lay on the bed, missing my ex-wife. When I'd been sick, she always nursed me back to good health. When I'd been lonely, Priyanka married me. When I'd wanted a child, she'd given birth to Freya.

When I'd been broke, Priyanka had pushed me to become successful.

She'd given me everything a woman could give, yet it was never enough.

The grass was always greener on the other side. I'd had the perfect woman and I'd left her. I would break into a country-and-western song if I continued moping.

When I saw Freya every Sunday, Priyanka would be out or she would open the door and remain behind it to avoid seeing me. Who could blame her? Twenty-one years of devotion and I left her due to my failing battle with poor mental health, terrible decision-making and depression.

She was the first woman who'd ever given a damn about me. Maybe in my previous life, I'd been a devious scumbag or a politician and this was my comeuppance.

Work suffered and I couldn't pay attention. I had to see what women wanted in men.

The equatorial weather became a week of rain and thunderstorms. So it was back to a typical British August. I arrived at the bar. It was socially distanced, nobody wore masks and it was Friday night. Some women were with girlfriends, others were with boyfriends. I ordered my drink and looked at the men who were spoken for. Who were they and how did they do it?

Ninety-five per cent of the men were white. Five per cent were cool black men or bad-boy Europeans. Not an Asian or Indian man in sight.

The white men were taller and skinnier than me.

The black men were taller and obviously worked out.

The Eastern Europeans (judging by their accents) were macho with a hint of mystery.

I'm an open book with the torn pages falling out. All the odds were stacked against me. How was I supposed to succeed in this environment?

The women didn't wish they were somewhere else with a bald, middle-aged Indian man. They were relaxed, chatty, laughing, not a worry in the world. I hadn't come here to stare, so I made an effort. If you don't try, you'll never know.

I hovered at the side of the bar. "Excuse me," said a lovely voice behind me.

I turned around. She had a lovely smile and a friendly face.

"Hi, I'm Niraj, and you are …?"

"Wanting to get past," she said, gliding by to the ladies' room. Oh, God, I was standing outside the ladies' like a pervert.

I moved to the middle of the bar. A woman my age with her hair in plaits and a low-cut top was waiting for her drinks. She caught me staring at her reflection in the mirror. I didn't know what to do so looked everywhere else.

"You come here often?" she asked.

She smiled and there was hope in her eyes, like she had been waiting for a man to have the courage to speak to her – and that man was me. It was the worst pickup line ever and it worked on me.

Except it didn't.

She rushed to the man behind me, who she was clearly talking to. He kissed her on the lips, right in my face. I grimaced and moved along.

A blonde woman who clearly worked out and was happy to show off her hard-earned assets was doing shots with her brunette friend who clearly didn't work out. Both in their early thirties. The blonde was out of my league, so I approached the brunette who had more zest for life.

"Hi, I'm Niraj Kapur, I'm new in town. Where's a good place to go?"

Don't know why I said that. I've lived here eighteen years. I was panicking, but it worked.

"Welcome to MK," said the brunette in a friendly voice. "Check out Willen Lake, it's wicked it is, and the indoor ski centre is mental. I'm Sarah."

"No! I just got my heart broken by a Sarah. Can I call you Brian?"

Don't know why I said that.

Brunette Sarah laughed, then a strange thing happened. Her blonde friend played with her hair and interrupted us. "I'm Lily," she said.

I ignored her, addressing Brunette Sarah. "Does she ever stop talking?"

Brunette Sarah sniggered. Lily gave me a disapproving look. *Join the queue, darling. Every woman disapproves of me these days.*

"I'm looking to meet some lovely blondes," I said, glancing at Lily then back at Brunette Sarah. "You don't know where I can find any, do you?"

If Lily had had laser beams for eyes, she would have burned me. I've never behaved like this before, but the power I seemed to have over her was incredible. Lily marched into the ladies', her high heels digging into the floor.

"Everybody wants a blonde. Try something different," Brunette Sarah said, leaning in. "You'll never know unless you try, d'ya know what I mean?"

Brunette Sarah was super-friendly but short and stocky with black lipstick, and excessive make-up doesn't do it for me.

Five minutes later, Lily exited the ladies'. Her lipstick was extra red and she smelled of perfume. She sashayed across the floor to get my attention. Men noticed her, judging by their eyes opening like a flower. One man got nudged by his jealous girlfriend.

"Thanks for the company, Sarah."

Brunette Sarah blew me a kiss. "Good luck, young man."

"Young man. You're officially the most awesome woman in this bar," I said. I meant it. Then I turned to Lily. "All the best, Billy."

Lily growled and I could hear her high heels clicking as she followed me. I don't know why I said that, I just wanted to wind her up. "You're a wanker!" she barked.

I stopped to listen to her. "Have you been talking to my ex-wife?" I said.

Before she could reply, I walked away again, driving her mad.

Lily must have been thinking, *why is he ignoring me? I'm the hottest woman in this bar! If Da Vinci was still alive, he would ask me to sit still and do his magic.*

"I do pilates! I hit the gym four times a week!" Lily said, turning to the side, giving me a profile view of her perfectly sculpted body.

I stopped and was impressed. Lily was all fired up. I could feel her rage and passion. She wanted me and all I had to do was be an asshole and ignore her. Our eyes locked.

"There's no cellulite on this baby," she told me.

"Prove it."

Thirty minutes later, we were in bed after an intense, beautiful session. We lay on our backs, satisfied. Lily cuddled up to me. I didn't cuddle back. I was enjoying my power.

No more Mr Nice Guy. Every time I'm nice to women, they cheat, lie and treat me badly. They rarely take my feelings into consideration, which is ironic when you think about how much women complain about men not taking their feelings into consideration.

If you want to achieve greatness, you have to become somebody different. I was now bad-boy Niraj who doesn't give a damn about you. I will not be tamed and you can't tie me down.

I'm doing this for middle-aged men everywhere with no voice. Overweight men. Introverted men. Indian men. Unattractive men. Men who have had their hearts broken.

This was the new me and women are one hundred per cent to blame for it.

After a quick clean-up, I slipped on my clothes.

"Are you going to call me?" asked Lily, hopeful.

"I'll think about it," I replied, avoiding eye contact.

Lily got on her knees, pleading. "Please, Niraj, I want to see you again."

She wanted me. She craved me. I had discovered the ancient secret of making a woman want me.

Being a bastard actually works. I've refused to do that in the past since it's not who I am. I treat women with respect and kindness because that's how I want to be treated. Look where respect, decency and kindness have got me.

Nowhere. Lonelytown. Depression Alley. Mental Health Road.

Not bothering to say goodbye, I opened the bedroom door. A tall macho man with stubble and several neck tattoos greeted me with a frown. He wasn't stylish enough to be a bouncer. More like a hitman or thug out on parole. "Where you going?" he asked in a deep and intimidating voice.

Every man dreams of a threesome. But not this kind of threesome. I retreated to the bed.

"Rocco, I got this," said Lily, changing her personality. She was taking control and slipped on her silk dressing gown.

"Rocco … isn't that the name you give a pit bull?" I thought to myself.

"You made me work hard, Niraj. Break his fingers, Rocco. He won't be able to write his next book!"

"How the hell did she know? Wait a minute, break my what now…?" I wondered.

"Niraj Kapur, I googled you while I was in the bathroom. You've written some sad stories about your dating history and loneliness. Then you put on that little act. Even I was almost fooled!"

"This is England, we can be civilised about this," I said, as calmly as I could under the current circumstances. "Rocco, come here please."

Rocco slowly stepped in. I made a break for it and leapt for the open bedroom door. Rocco stuck out his arm, grabbing my shirt, and flung me with such brute force I landed on the bed then dropped onto the floor with a thud.

Close your eyes, play dead … I said to myself.

Rocco took out a Swiss army knife and unlocked the corkscrew.

"No, no wait, hang on ..." I had no way out. So I played my last card. "Prostitution is illegal!"

"That's so crude. I'll have you know I'm a professional escort."

I didn't say it was a great card.

"You could still get arrested," I reminded her.

"Go ahead and call the police," Lily said, signalling to Rocco with a glance. He grabbed my arm and twisted. It was excruciating. "Snap his writing hand," Lily ordered him.

"No, that's my second-favourite organ," I begged them. "What do you want?"

"Your credit card," said Lily, like she'd done it a thousand times. "We go to a cashpoint, take out £500, then you're free to go." She fumbled through my wallet, took out my driver's licence and took a picture on her mobile.

"If you call the police, we know where you live."

I had no choice. I thought I was being smart by being the bastard. Turns out a fool is always a fool.

Lily gave me back my mobile. It had stopped ringing. "Take a good look in the mirror," she said, leading me to her full-length mirror. I hated what I saw staring back at me: a humiliation of a man.

"Men like you don't have happy endings," said Lily.

She was right. I'd tried to break the rules and the rules ended up breaking me. Pretty white people always win.

We drove to the cashpoint. Rocco stood over me in the dark. I typed in £500. It made me feel physically sick as the money came out of my account. I'd worked so hard to earn that cash and now it was wasted because I'd wanted to show off.

I gave Rocco the £500. He checked it, shoved it into his back pocket, gave me an army salute and strutted away.

I didn't know what to say or do. Lily was right. Men like me don't have a happy ending. I was proof that no matter how hard you try in life, you never get anywhere.

Business Lesson Learned

Trust your gut. You can use software to analyse so much. You can have advisors guide you in the right direction. Sometimes you need to spend moments thinking about things, rather than rushing into them. When you see a warning sign, it doesn't make a loud noise or wave its arms in front of you. Sometimes it's a hunch. Other times it happens and you ignore it.

Don't ignore the warning signs. If something is too good to be true, it usually is. If you ignore these, the consequences can be dangerous.

"Too many people listen to the noise of the world, instead of themselves." – Germany Kent

Chapter 12

TAKING A BREAK

I wolfed down my trusted Ben & Jerry's Phish Food. For the first time ever, it did nothing for me. I tried a packet of KitKat Chunkies. Nothing. After a sugar nap, I woke up again, had fish and chips. Nothing. Went back for more fish and chips. Stomach felt like it was going to rip open. I was sick. Fell asleep. Had motivation to do nothing.

Repeat. Day after day. A month later, I was in constant food comas. Migraines were burning my head 24/7 from excessive sugar in my bloodstream. My right knee was causing me to limp. I went to the doctor and was diagnosed "obese".

As a child, I was sporty and weight was never an issue.

In my twenties, I could have eaten smarter, had a more toned belly, although it was nothing too bad.

In my late forties, losing weight was hell. You put it on so easy and exercise doesn't give you any kind of thrill.

Waiting lists on the NHS can be extreme. Luckily, they had a last-minute cancellation and I filled the spot. The diagnosis came back a few days later: "osteoarthritis in your right knee".

I facetimed my parents from my laptop and told them what had happened.

They insisted I return home to heal. I needed to be around family and get some stability in my life in Northern Ireland.

"I've lived in England for twenty-nine years. This is my home!"

"Northern Ireland will always be your home," Dad reminded me. Your sister and brother are there. Your friend Alan who looks like a hippopotamus is there. Your childhood friend DJ …"

"Dad, 'JJ'. For God's sake, it's JJ! For forty-eight years it's been JJ. Get it right. You were a heart surgeon."

Dad must have taken that for my pain talking, because he didn't yell back or tell me to watch my manners. "Did you know the first people on earth were Indian?"

"I thought Adam and Eve were the first people on earth."

"Did you know the second people on earth were Indian?" my father continued. "We created chess, ink, flush toilets and Cliff Richard." He opened up the Bhagavad Gita, the Indian version of the Bible where a Post-it note was sticking out. "A season of grieving may be necessary, but a lifetime of grieving isn't," he said.

I clapped slowly and sarcastically. As usual, religion has so much to say and says nothing.

"It's time for you to come home," Mum said softly.

What kind of forty-eight-year-old man lives with his parents? Quite simply, one that has failed miserably in life. At my age, I should be taking care of my parents and sending them on well-deserved holidays to enjoy the rest of their retirement. They should not be supporting their screwed-up son who tried hard at life and failed horribly.

I called Freya from my mobile, put her on loudspeaker and asked her thoughts on me moving back to Northern Ireland and put my mobile on a loudspeaker.

"Cool," she replied. Young people today really are masters of the art of conversation.

"That's it?" I asked, hoping for anything more.

"I know what you're like, Dad. You've already made your mind up. You're just like your own father …"

"No need to insult me, young lady!" interrupted Dad, whose manner always became more playful around his granddaughter.

"Grandad, hey, good to hear from you! How are you? How's Grandma? How's the charity work?" Freya said, cheering up.

That was more than she normally says to me in an hour. I get "Cool" and a long pause. Being a grandparent is all of the perks and none of the responsibility.

Dad found an estate agent on Google, although he couldn't make it until the following day. Dad reminded him that he was a doctor, a humanitarian and had won the MBE. The estate agent made it to my house within the hour! Unbelievable.

Self-pity and loneliness would lead to mental health problems again. If I went down that dark and dangerous road, I would end up in hospital or six feet under.

This house had so many memories. It was where Freya grew up. Where we took pictures on her first day of primary school. Where she had birthday parties, from clowns entertaining the kids to parents being banned because we were so embarrassing. Freya had sleepovers with the same loyal and amazing friends she'd had since she was three years old.

We could only afford one car. When Priyanka eventually

bought her own car, it was broken into and the CD player stolen. The fear brought us closer together.

Priyanka had painted the rooms and decorated it with elegance. She made the most delicious Indian meals, the kind of dishes you can't have on the streets of India since you will get food poisoning there with the tap water. I know, I've had Delhi Belly on several occasions and it takes almost a week to recover. The house always smelled of Indian food or fresh homemade bread, another wonderful skill Priyanka had.

This was where Priyanka and I had dreamed of a bigger and better life. It was where Priyanka had started her business and where I'd discovered personal development, which changed my world.

Despite the pain of the divorce, we did have some lovely moments and memories. Priyanka was a great voice of reason. She'd been strong through every moment in my life and I wished she was here now.

Finally, I packed my photo albums. The friends I'd made over the decades. The business connections. The business cards from the conferences I've attended. The memories … everything is online now. The world is so uncertain and nobody knows what will happen tomorrow. We're connected through social media, yet we're so disconnected as a human race.

If everyone is online, why stay here? Why not go back home to Northern Ireland? At least I will be with my parents and never feel lonely or isolated from the world. When I'm in pain, I can get a wonder hug from my mother.

So I made a list of the pros and cons of living with my parents.

Cons:

- ✗ I'd lose my privacy.
- ✗ I'd have to start over. For twenty-nine years I built my career in England.
- ✗ My old room used to be adorned with posters of Cindy Crawford, Elisabeth Shue and Tom Cruise. Now it has statues of Lord Krishna and Indian gods, where incense burns and the bookshelves contain volumes on Gandhi, Mother Teresa, Wayne Dyer's *Spirituality* and *How to Become a Better Human.*
- ✗ That meant I'd have to live in my sister's old room, which still had lots of my sister's stuff there.

Pros:

- ✓ Mum would cook fresh food for me instead of me eating greasy, fattening takeaways.
- ✓ She would give me hugs every morning, which is great for my soul and mental health.
- ✓ I'd cut my expenses by at least £3,000 a month, my friends were nearby, neighbours would pop in for a chat and I could pick up my nephew from school.
- ✓ Many of my friends had lost their fathers in recent years due to prostate cancer or Parkinson's. I'm so lucky and grateful mine was still alive, even though he was often two sandwiches short of a picnic.
- ✓ More importantly, it would help me recover from the divorce, losing my business and the trauma of living alone and having nobody to share my life with.

Everything I owned went into storage and I took home a suitcase of books, laptop and clothes and my phone.

Before leaving for Northern Ireland, I dropped Freya back at Warwick University.

When her car broke down, I was always there. When she needed a lift at 3 a.m. from the nightclub, I was always happy to pick Freya and her friends up and drop them home, knowing they would be safer than being in some random taxi. Despite the closer bond she had with her mum, Freya knew she could always rely on me to be there.

Your child leaving home is a scary moment in life, especially when you have no other children or family nearby. At least I saw her every fortnight. I would pick her up from student accommodation and bring her home to get her clothes washed. When your children grow up, you don't see them as much. However, Freya was still my baby girl. She was the light of my life and the best thing that had ever happened to me. I planned to see her at Christmas, but three months away from your child hurts, no matter what age they are.

"Just because I'm not here, doesn't mean I'm not with you," I promised her.

"You shouldn't drink and drive," she replied, in her usual dry manner.

Like my father, she didn't say "I love you", rarely gave hugs and wasn't the nurturing kind. Like my ex-wife, she made intelligent decisions and was able to keep emotion out of the equation. An incredible gift, although as her father, I wanted hugs all the time.

We carried the suitcases to the top of her shared house, walking up the narrowest of stairs, which creaked like it was a haunted house. After I helped her unpack, it was time to say goodbye. I had taken £250 from the cash machine. I gave it to her.

"Yay, I have money to get drunk," she said, deadpan, flicking through the money.

I knew Freya would use the excuse of social distancing to avoid hugging me goodbye. I had no recent photographs of her as she didn't like having her photo taken. So I took one last look. This amazing girl had practically brought herself up, while her parents were working long hours to pay the bills.

Every parent says their child is the smartest. I have her report cards to prove that she is. This straight-A student was now a young woman in her final year. She looked and acted like my ex-wife. She had hair like my mother's, when my mother was young, and a face like my sister. She was addicted to her phone and could easily go for days without talking to another human being, while I love socialising with people. My God, did we have nothing in common?

"I'll fly over at Christmas and see you," I said, before turning to leave. Freya never did soppy goodbyes. As I opened the front door, she surprised me by wrapping her arms around me. "Don't forget to write to me like an old person," she said.

It was the first proper hug she'd given me in years. It was like she was saying, "It's okay, Dad, I've got this. Please take care of yourself. I'm never going to tell you how I feel. Just know I'll always be your girl and that I'll always be thinking about you."

I didn't want Freya to see me cry. Your child will never know how much you truly love them until they become parents themselves.

I was only on a ferry once as a kid, with the Cub Scouts.

Cairnryan in west Scotland to Larne in the east of Northern Ireland by ferry was only two hours, compared to the Liverpool to Belfast ferry which was eight hours on an overnight trip.

The 400-mile drive to west Scotland might as well have been 1,000 miles since it took all day. During the eight-hour drive, I tried to think of a solution to my problems and couldn't. At my age, you're supposed to know what to do with your life, yet I hadn't a clue what to do next.

All I did know was that after twenty-nine years in England, nobody said goodbye. Not. One. Single. Person. No matter how you look at it, that is a social failure of epic proportions. People knew what I had endured, but they were too busy trying to cope with their own issues, or didn't care or didn't want to get involved.

This is one of the biggest regrets of my life, not having a tribe around me or friends I could talk with. Life was family and work. Nothing else.

I stopped at several service stations along the way to stretch my legs, have more paracetamol and yet another soy latte to keep me awake. Lots of thoughts were racing through my mind.

Was I making the right decision? Was I rushing? Why, after investing £20,000 on personal development, mindset and business events, courses and books, was I in such a mess?

I'm a forty-eight-year-old man about to move back in with his parents. My whole life I'd been knocked down and found the strength to get back on my feet. Sometimes it took a few days, sometimes a few weeks.

There was no getting up from this. Dating had ruined me. Divorce had knocked me out. Going back home, it felt like I was giving up.

Sea air is calm and soothing on the skin. You breathe in that lovely fresh air and the world makes sense … except it was bloody freezing and the behemoth of a ferry was shaking side to side, thanks to the autumn winds and rough waters. Due to social distancing, people were meant to be sitting apart, but they were too close together, so I was up on deck, staring at the ocean with a huge knot in my stomach.

Uber had been created because the founder couldn't get a taxi in Paris. Airbnb was founded when people needed help with the high rent prices in San Francisco. Netflix disrupted Blockbuster. Amazon disrupted bookstores. I've read extensively about these large corporations.

People wanted something that didn't exist, so they went out and created it.

What could I create that would help me cope with online dating?

What about a virtual-reality headset where I could see Priyanka in my head and always have her with me? That was actually not a bad idea, but I didn't know how to create that. I'm not a visionary, in that sense. I have no desire to be rich or change the world. I'm a man that has lost his true love and wants her back. I just want all this pain to go away.

There was a sudden dip in the ocean and a large wave caused the ferry to shake. The captain made an announcement and other people on deck rushed inside.

I didn't leave. What if I was swept out to sea? What if I jumped overboard?

I put my foot on the first railing. I could hear people inside freaking out as the ferry hit another swell in the sea.

What did I have to live for? Freya was grown up, surrounded

by amazing friends, her grandparents and my ex-wife. She would be fine. I'd always been curious to know what heaven was like. Suicide wasn't selfish if done for the right reasons.

I climbed up to the second rail. What would it be like in heaven? I would take poetry classes from Shakespeare, attend Robin Williams' comedy events, learn about charity from Mother Teresa. There would be no war, no famine, no cruel dictators, no lockdown, no incompetent government, no loneliness, no greedy businesses, no financial worries. Heaven has to be better than earth.

I put my foot on the third rail. Now my legs were getting weak. Was that a sign to dive in? I was nervous and that didn't stop me wanting to jump.

"Get your arse inside," said a man in a strong Scottish accent. He could have been security or another passenger. I never saw his face. He grabbed me by the collar and dragged me inside. I'm seventeen stone and my feet scuffed the deck, so I wasn't about to argue.

I planned to go to my car, lower my car seat and take the opportunity to sleep. Normally a good rest makes me feel better. But with the stormy seas and rolling ferry, I went instead to the toilet, where I was sick for the next hour.

My Irish neighbours were different to my English ones. Over the years, Dad had treated them, their kids and their relatives at the health centre, so I was treated with love. It took me twenty minutes to get to the front door. "How are ye?", "Welcome back, wee man!" and my favourite: "My my, you've got a lot bigger since we last saw ye."

I was dazed by all that had happened. Mum didn't say anything. She didn't have to. Her warm embrace was enough.

She held on tight and I melted in her arms. For such a tiny woman, she had amazing healing powers. She made my favourite dessert: homemade fruit trifle with jelly, fresh custard and finely chopped apple, pear and peaches.

Dad had been to get a fresh sourdough loaf from the bakery and local honey from the butcher. Imagine a vegetarian walking into the butcher's? That's where the best local honey was and Dad knew I loved honey. My father was old school. He didn't say "I love you". He didn't wear his heart on his sleeve. He was a good man with his charity talk, but expressing his emotions wasn't for him.

He put his hand on my shoulder. It stayed there a moment. If there was ever a time for him to say that he loved me, it was now. "Put on the kettle, would you?" he said.

My nephews popped round and immediately set on me, kneeing me in the balls in the process.

Despite that pain, it was lovely to see them. My sister gave me a meditation CD and my brother brought more carbs in the shape of a twelve-inch Subway sandwich: my favourite consisting of chicken, cheese, mayo and as much salad as you could stuff inside.

What would have happened if I'd jumped from the ship?

I'm so glad that stranger stopped me. My parents would have been devastated. How would my siblings feel? Here I am surrounded by people who care. In the heat of the moment, with emotions running high, it's so easy to make a stupid decision.

Business Lesson Learned

Sometimes no matter how hard you try, things don't go your way. Taking a break is key. Walking away from the misery and pain is vital.

You rarely make smart decisions when angry or depressed. England had been the country of my dreams. It's where I became a dad and had a career. Now it was over. I had to start again. It broke my heart that I couldn't make things work.

Taking a break is important. Slow down. Work on your thinking. It gives you more clarity. Surround yourself with people who care. Take up a new hobby. We all need a break from work and life when things don't go our way.

Chapter 13

SELF-CARE

When I woke up, I checked my phone. Nobody from England asked how I was or how I was settling in. Shame.

I had breakfast with Mum and Dad. It was so lovely to have people in the house to talk to.

"What are your plans?" Dad asked.

I didn't know.

"I have something next door for you," Dad said and continued eating his toast and marmalade.

"Please tell me it's another arranged marriage," I joked.

My parents were confused. They never understood my sarcasm.

Dad had kindly bought me a work chair and comfy desk. There was a notepad, pens and colourful Post-it notes on my desk, along with some books on God. Rick Warren's *What On Earth Am I Here For?* and several different ones by Indian philosopher J. P. Vaswani. I believe there's a God who created earth, although I'm not sure why he allows so many bad things to happen.

When you're in pain, you often think you're the only one

going through it. Other people have often gone through what you have and there's no shame in asking for help. I had to rebuild my life again and figured a therapist would be the best way to start. I arrived at the therapist's garage, which had been converted into a workspace. I paid for the hour and got ready to heal.

Therapist:	What do you hate about your parents?
Me:	(confused) I love my parents.
Therapist:	You need to write what you hate about your parents and then burn the letter.
Me:	Maybe you weren't listening. I get on great with my parents, the problem is the divorce. My married friends don't get me. I'm lonely. It has nothing to do with my parents.
Therapist:	This is how I help my patients. You need to purge your childhood pain.
Me:	Just to clarify, there's about 500 million Indian men in the world with little hair and funny accents. Don't suppose you got one of us mixed up?
Therapist:	This is how I do things. There's a process to everything.

The therapist didn't listen and only cared about her own agenda.

Two minutes later, I told her what I thought of her and left. So much for therapy.

I grew up in a pleasant middle-class area of a rough working-class town called Antrim. Being Indian I never fitted in. I considered myself Irish, the locals considered me an immigrant. Offensive words like "Paki", "Fag" and "Negro" were regularly thrown at me in school.

As you can imagine, I wasn't comfortable in my own skin, became deeply insecure and found it hard to trust anyone.

That's why I left home at eighteen and moved to London. Nobody cared what colour I was. There's a wonderful comfort in that.

Now I would walk into cafes in Antrim with my laptop. Some people would stare like they've never seen a person of colour in their lives. I didn't wear a fancy business suit, long hair or have offensive tattoos, yet here I was being judged by the same small-minded people I grew up with. They stared, and I mean stared, like my colour offended them. Also, I was usually the only person in the cafe with a laptop and coloured skin, but that's not the point.

A wonderful cup of coffee and Victoria sponge cake usually makes life better. In small-town Northern Ireland it doesn't. They just judged, then ignored.

So I needed to find better ways to heal. This is what I did:

- I went into nature every morning for thirty minutes. Phone off. There were lots of people walking dogs. Some said hello, some didn't. All women avoided eye contact. Sometimes I smiled and said hello. Twenty per cent of the time they replied. Eighty per cent of the time they ignored me. So much for the Irish charm. I ended up avoiding the busy paths to avoid people and went into the quieter areas. Listened to birds sing. Appreciated the green beauty all around me and the flowing of rivers. The squirrels playing. The dogs being walked. Animals are so much nicer than humans.

- Discovered a wonderful comedy called *Parks and Recreation* on Amazon Prime. What a joy. I rarely watch TV, so this was a true gem about community, togetherness and friendship, something that was desperately lacking in my life.
- Bought myself something special every week. I allow £20 per week no questions asked and it can't be for work. Purchases that have cheered me up include: a yoga mat, a box of delicious handmade chocolates and second-hand rock shirts.
- Took my time writing in my gratitude journal. Every night, I write down five things I'm grateful for. No matter how tough things get, gratitude makes life easier. When you have a bad day and you're all alone, finding things to be grateful for is even more important. I have heating in my house, three meals a day, fresh water to drink and a roof over my head.
- Gave regularly to charity. I didn't have much money to give, so I gave my time and expertise in sales and marketing. The more you give, the more you live. It's good for your soul. Also, the good you put out in the world comes back to you, or so I've been told.
- Had a warm bath with Epsom salts, with the phone turned off and candles lit. One of life's great joys. Like many things, it's strange at first and you lie there wondering what do. Silence is your friend. Enjoy it.
- Digital detox once a week, and turn all apps and emails off at least twice a day. Technology is wonderful, but it will cause damage to your focus, mental health and expectations of life, if you can't control it.

- No holding grudges. This is a tough one. It's not easy forgiving those who have done us wrong. It's difficult to forgive people who have hurt you and even those who have ignored you. Learning to forgive, let go and be at peace takes time.
- Read *The Comfort Book* by Matt Haig. The best investment I made, more valuable than any therapist. Too many books focus on science and research and it's not that interesting. *The Comfort Book* tells it like it is and life begins to make more sense.
- Eating better. Getting off my addiction to sugar was like a drug addict getting off cocaine. It's all you can think about. Food tastes amazing and you crave it, especially when you're on a diet. I had no reason to comfort eat and Mum made delicious fresh Indian food of every kind, not that chicken tikka nonsense you get in restaurants, the kind of delicious soul food you can't get in the UK unless you venture into Southall, Wembley or Leicester.
- Spiritual health. I started to get into Rick Warren's *What On Earth Am I Here For?* That was mind-blowing. It was about talking to God and making him your friend and when you have God, you are never alone. That was a big surprise. Talk to Him through the day and think about how amazing it will be in heaven. It's important to have a high faith in something bigger than you.
- Lastly, physical health. This should be your first choice; however, I got to it last. Just before Christmas I joined the gym to get into shape. The better your physical health, the better you can manage your mental health. Two weeks after I joined, we went into a five-month lockdown.

As humans, we want to be heard, to be understood and to be respected. We also need hugs, which are wonderful for mental health, and sex, which is vital to make you feel alive. It burns as many calories as the gym, and let's be real, it's WAY more fun than the gym.

Five more months of lockdown slowly dragged me back towards a dangerous place, a place I refused to go back to again.

Business Lesson Learned

Self-care reduces the stress in your life. You become less frustrated and less irritated with others. You can't help anyone unless you can help yourself. This is a small chapter although it's possibly the most important one in the book. Please reread it, underline/make notes and, most importantly, take action.

Self-care is strange when you're a man. It's not discussed in the pub. You're not taught it at school and it never came up in my marriage or at any work learning day. When you're able to take care of yourself, you can take care of others, in the office and at home.

"To love oneself is the beginning of a lifelong romance." – Oscar Wilde

Chapter 14

VULNERABILITY

When you have amazing success, some people want to be you, although many resent you. They think you had it lucky, they think you sucked up to or, even worse, slept with the right person or stabbed the right people in the back.

With vulnerability, you're not bragging or showing off. There's all kinds of science and research on this, from vulnerability being good for your emotional and physical health to being a sign of courage.

In my case, it helps people understand me. It also allowed my voice to be heard in ways I never expected.

LinkedIn is a business-to-business social media platform, the largest in the world with 650 million users in 2021. It would later rise to 830 million users in summer 2022.

Most people spoke about business back then. So did I. Then one day I changed direction.

After months of working on self-care, I slowly rebuilt my life. Everything in baby steps. My mental health improved. My physical health got slightly better. I became closer to God. My panic attacks reduced. Three months feels like forever sometimes and it did. When the second lockdown hit, my business content started getting noticed. More views, more likes, more comments. People sent me private messages saying they liked my content and wanted coaching. People I'd helped years ago to find work, or given advice to on sales, reached out to say they needed sales training.

Money started coming in. Government loans were reduced. Overdraft disappeared. Credit cards disappeared ... and I poured everything into my career.

It was a proud moment to regrow my business from nothing to profit in such a short time. There was one major problem.

I had nobody to share it with.

It's inhuman to work fifteen to sixteen hours a day, seven days a week – at the same time, I was putting in twelve hours a day, sometimes fourteen hours. The rest of the time was spent bonding with Mum and Dad and helping out around the house.

On Saturdays I would walk in nature. I couldn't indulge in any coffee shops since everything was shut. Libraries shut. Bookshops. The whole world was shut. I wasn't asking for an unrealistic relationship with a skinny, rich celebrity or to live a laptop lifestyle in luxury by the beach with passive income.

I simply wanted someone to share my life with.

That's it. Nothing complex. Not high expectations. Simply a common bond of kindness, laughter, love, good music and wanting to make the world a better place through charity work. Turns out the simplest things are actually rather complex to find.

So I rejoined Match, Bumble and Plenty of Fish and tried out Tinder. I'm a different person now so should enjoy dating more.

Wrong. Nobody wants to meet up due to fear of Covid. Not for coffee. Not for a walk. For nothing.

There's a LOT of women online who want to talk. For months. They never want to meet up. I will let Covid take some of that responsibility.

When you spend two hours every single night on dating apps, it's hard work trying to connect with people you don't know. At my age, women have lots of baggage. They're often going through big changes with menopause. Their marriages are over; some are forced by their friends to go dating; others are looking for a quick fix. Their teenage children drive them crazy and they often have ex-partners who are completely useless or total psychos.

Men are criticised for cheating, but guess what? They usually cheat with a woman, which makes women just as guilty.

I reached breaking point when the situation below happened. I wrote about it on LinkedIn and it became my first viral post.

Start of post.

"I feel sorry for you." That's what my childhood friend said to me on Sunday when I bumped into her grocery shopping.

She put her arm on my shoulder. "I saw you sitting in the McDonald's car park on Saturday night by yourself. You looked so upset."

"Why didn't you say hello?" I asked, curiously.

"Oh, you know, I had things to do. The whole community has been talking about you, Niraj. It must be so difficult being single at your age and living with your parents."

I bit my lip, a habit to tell myself to not react too quickly.

I'm proud of rebuilding my business after losing my clients in the first lockdown. I'm proud that after two years of battling mental health from my divorce, my confidence and health is in good shape in 2021. No matter how much pain I've suffered, I never stopped helping people or giving to charities.

At the same time, I'm human.

- ✗ Sitting alone in a car park on a Saturday night is unbearable.
- ✗ The experiences I had with online dating were awful.
- ✗ There's so many terrible dating coaches I spent £££ on who told me "believe and it will happen" and "don't chase anyone, let them find you". None of which work.
- ✗ Three years of not being with anyone special is going to really f**king hurt from time to time.

"Do you remember your wedding day?" I asked.

"Yes, that was such an amazing day," she cheered up.

"I was there. I flew over from England to attend. I've known you for thirty years. You have my mobile. Why didn't you call me and ask me how I was if you knew I was struggling?"

"I don't have your number," she replied far too quickly.

I easily found her number on my phone and pressed the green button. Her mobile rang. She immediately turned it off.

The longest, most painful pause followed. She hung her head in shame and left.

When people are hurting, don't gossip about them and don't ignore them. Here's what you do:

- ✓ Meet them face to face.
- ✓ If you can't, have a Zoom session.
- ✓ If you can't, pick up the phone and call them.
- ✓ Ask how they are. Not to give advice, just to listen.

✓ Remember that everyone wants to be listened to and have their voice heard.

The happiest people are not those who are lucky or born happy. They're the ones who have often dealt with the worst pain and know how unbearable it is to be alone in this world – so they do what they can to help others.

Kindness and patience cost nothing.

Gossip and ignorance cost everything.

End of post.

Men's mental health is often unspoken, uncomfortable or treated with pity as opposed to faced openly and compassionately, whether it's physical or psychological health.

Having a post go viral is something most people aspire to. Many believe it will solve their problems. This is like thinking winning the lottery will solve your problems. Seventy per cent of lottery winners end up broke and a third go on to declare bankruptcy, according to the National Endowment for Financial Education.

Going viral is wonderful for your ego. You gain thousands of followers and people recognise your voice. Here's what's more important:

The outpouring of love from people, many whom I had never spoken to, telling me it was going to be okay. That I would one day find love. It gave me hope. I was then inundated with hundreds of private messages from men telling me they're going through divorce and it's hell, but they work in industries like banking and logistics where these things cannot be discussed. They're grateful I was their voice. Others were inspired to talk about their pain thanks to me. Many introverts said they would never talk about this publicly and were grateful to me for doing so.

This was overwhelming. It was also a huge responsibility.

Then something happened that I never expected.

A client who had been reading my content for months reached out to say, "Your post was real and heartfelt. I'm looking for a coach and would like to have a chat. Are you available in the next week?" We arranged a meeting and I asked my six magic questions:

- ✓ What do you want to achieve?
- ✓ Why do you want to achieve it?
- ✓ What will it mean when you achieve it?
- ✓ On a scale of 1–10, how committed are you?
- ✓ What deadline are you working to?
- ✓ What happens if you do nothing?

You can never help anyone without asking questions. A doctor would never diagnose without asking what was wrong, that would get them fired for malpractice.

She gave me her answers. Then and only then did I tell her how I could help solve her problems with mindset work, a vision board, understanding sales process, learning how to write emails that clients respond to – and she became a paying client.

This was incredible. What if it was a one-off? After all, running a business is a marathon, not a sprint, which is ironic, since I used to be a sprinter at school.

A month later, I share a picture in a delicious Mexican

restaurant in Belfast, called Acapulco. I had a delicious burrito of spicy chicken and roast vegetables, with tortilla chips on the side. The seat opposite me was empty. The post read “Stood up again”.

I felt so embarrassed. It’s like getting ready to see a client. You get dressed up, so you prep. You’re a little nervous because you want everything to go right. The outcome can have an impact on your future. They don’t show up. They don’t even have the manners to call and apologise.

The outpouring of support from people publicly on LinkedIn was comforting. “Hang in there, mate.” “You deserve better and you will find true love, Niraj.” “You’re one step closer to finding the right person.”

My private LinkedIn messaging inbox was flooded with private messages of support and, yet again, another business contacted me. “Loved your post. Went back and read your other posts. Let’s talk, I need help with my sales.” A week later, another new client booked.

Every week I shared a dating story on LinkedIn. Why was I paying for all the first dates? How nervous I was. Not knowing what clothes to wear. A wonderful new restaurant find. Bumping into members of the Indian community on a date who didn’t know I was divorced and having them awkwardly stare at me. My sincerity connecting with people on social media.

Too many people brag about things that never happen to sound impressive. Others choose to be divisive and hateful to get attention. I was leading from the heart and baring my soul. Sales can be aggressive and has a terrible reputation. Here I was, a man teaching sales who was genuine, caring, honest, vulnerable, with no sleazy tactics or ulterior motive.

With success, comes the haters. They're all the same white angry men over fifty, who see everyone and everything as a threat. Their comments are too offensive to be repeated. The first time anything bad happens is always scary, so I asked my father for advice.

"Do you know this person?"

"No, Dad."

"Do you respect this person?

"Absolutely not, Dad."

"Then stop complaining. There's children starving in the world and, by the way, it wouldn't do you any harm to lose some weight."

I would add to that "block and report them" is also something you should do. It gives you peace of mind. Never waste your time arguing with someone beneath you.

Never engage with them. Never try and talk sense. As Mark Twain and many others have said, "Never wrestle with a pig. It gets mud all over you and the pig likes it."

Freya flew over to see me after lockdown lifted. I'd not seen her for almost eleven months. She hadn't been vaccinated yet, neither had my parents. Flying was risky, then she had her final university exams. When she arrived at Belfast International airport, I wanted to tell Freya how much I loved her and how I missed her; however, she doesn't do affection or hugs.

So I shook her hand; it was so polite and civilised, you know, British.

Taking her suitcase, I placed it in the boot. Then she wrapped her arms around me and said, "I miss you, Dad." I burst into tears. Eleven months of not seeing your child will take its toll. Even if that child doesn't say much and rarely calls, they're still your child and you still think about them all the time and pray for their safety and good health.

My family all took turns spending time with Freya and we didn't get much time to talk. Having her around the house was good enough. She was always there when I came into the kitchen to get a cup of herbal tea or have dinner. My parents were delighted to have their firstborn grandchild at home. She didn't say much, yet brought so much positive energy into the house. When we went out, the family surrounded her like a movie star, even though she wore normal clothes and treated everyone as equals.

I posted about my experiences seeing Freya again on LinkedIn.

Boom.

Another viral post.

So many people hadn't seen their parents in over a year, or not seen their grandparents because of this wretched virus. They related to what I was saying and I was overwhelmed with well wishes and support from business colleagues and people I'd never spoken to in my life, thanking me for respecting her boundaries and telling me I'm a great dad.

Yet again, I had several business enquiries. Thirty per cent converted to paying clients.

Business Lesson Learned:

Vulnerability matters. It allows people to see past your job title. It humanises you. Makes you more accessible and relatable. Shows your honesty. Shows your empathy. Helps you build deeper relationships. Vulnerability is never a weakness, it's a strength and it takes courage to open yourself up.

Vulnerability attracts more clients. More clients lead to more revenue, which often leads to more profits.

When I talk about vulnerability, many people say they will never discuss their private life or show pictures of their kids to get more noticed. I understand that and respect it. I'm simply sharing what works. You can be right or you can be successful. You can't always be both.

You also don't have to show every scar like I do. Talking about your struggles and how you overcame them makes you human.

People buy people.

Chapter 15

KNOW THE DECISION-MAKER

As the world slowly opened up due to lockdown measures being lifted, I got myself out there. Told several friends I've known for decades that I was available and wanted to meet single people. Dating in Northern Ireland is different to dating in England.

1) Women in Northern Ireland ask what religion you are. As offensive as I find that, it's common practice. Others are more discreet and ask, "What school did you go to?" They can then work out if you're Protestant or Catholic. It's clear from my profile pic I'm neither, which often led to another awkward question I was asked.

2) Were you born here? Like I'm an immigrant? Not that it should matter. In Northern Ireland it does. These aren't women living sheltered lives in the countryside, these are women from Belfast who have proper jobs and a university education.

3) We had more lockdowns than the rest of the UK, so most

women didn't want to meet up. This went on forever. Video dating isn't the same. You want to be there in the moment. To feel the energy. Hold a hand. The smell of perfume or shampoo. It adds to the senses and makes the dating experience more enjoyable.

4) You get ignored more on dating profiles. There is a peace process, no terrorism, and gay marriages are finally legal although it's one of the latest countries in the UK to allow it. As for skin colour, it's a major problem. It didn't depress me. It just disappointed me. Just because you're an island doesn't mean you live isolated from the world.

My first intro was Roisin. She was a single mum with grown-up kids. Slender, early fifties, had hair like it was still the 1980s and claimed to be a good craic. Just to clarify, the word "craic" means fun on Irish shores. She was convinced "I wouldn't be accepted by her family of staunch Protestants." Wow, I didn't even get a phone call or date.

That was one of my better experiences.

I bumped into my childhood friend, Ursula, in Tesco. I'd not seen her since primary school and she recognised me instantly. In primary school, she had braces due to her buck teeth and black NHS glasses. Now she was a charming and funny tomboy who owned a chain of successful car shops. She asked me if I'd like to go back to her place. I agreed and we spent all night talking about cars. She loved them. Fast cars, old cars, classic cars. She had raced Porsches, was obsessed with *Top Gear* reruns and attended car festivals several times a year.

She had been stalking me online for a few years, yet never

reached out. Then she invited me to her place for spaghetti bolognese, the ultimate comfort food.

As the night progressed, her lips approached mine. I could feel her breath on my skin, her fingers tickling my neck, then she tried to upsell to me an Audi Q7. When I objected, she tried to downsell me to an Audi A4. As I left the house, she offered an Audi A3. When I arrived home, she texted me a picture of an Audi A1 on special offer.

Kiera was a university professor teaching business, introduced through someone who bought my first book, *Everybody Works in Sales*. Kiera was a coffee snob; tick. She didn't shop at Lidl or Asda and preferred M & S; tick. We met at Holohan's at the Barge in Belfast, which I was told had cracking views of the city. When I arrived, it had a bridge, not like London Bridge, just a bridge and a tall building. Not the tallest building in the world or a fancy-shaped building, just a building. Luckily, the food was ace. Kiera was elegant, snobby and had no time for foreplay.

"Do you like pineapple on pizza?"

I was taken back by her abruptness. "Nice to meet you, too."

"Yes or no to pineapple?" she insisted, her fingers impatiently tapping her forearm.

"One hundred per cent yes. Everything tastes better with pineapple, especially pizza."

She gave me a playful high five and we ordered two meat pizzas with pineapple. Once she ate a slice, she popped a pill. "For anxiety attacks."

"Sorry to hear that. What happened?"

"My ex. Lots of scary men out there." She took another bite of pizza and popped a pill from a different bottle. "I have diabetes." She went on for a while. Eat a piece of pizza, then another pill, and another.

For once, I said I didn't think we were the right fit. She seemed upset and I felt awful. I was starting to wonder if I'd ever meet anyone again.

Gosia was recommended to me by Terri, an old school friend. Terri had wild ginger hair, tattoos and worked in HR, where her tattoos were covered up. She got in touch via Facebook, asked how I was and said that she had a friend, Gosia, who I might be interested in.

Gosia was going to be shopping in Belfast and would I be interested in meeting up?

I asked Terri what Gosia was like. "She's beautiful, you'll get on so well, so you will," she said.

What men find beautiful and what women find beautiful are vastly different.

According to *Next Luxury*, a magazine for the modern gentleman, this is a selection of what women find attractive in men: grooming (I wear tailored clothes), smell (I wash every day and use quality products and aftershave), following his plans (I'm a coach, I practise what I teach), a sense of adventure in bed (I don't want to brag), kindness to strangers (always) and cleanliness in the home (my cleaner does that, but I take the point).

The only two aspects I miss out on are height (I'm not that tall at 5 foot, 8 inches) and smile (I have vampire teeth at the side, so my smile is awkward).

What do men like about women? There's some terrible answers out there, from head tilt to high-pitched voice (which men are making these choices?). Boobs, bottom, kindness and a smile. You won't go far wrong with those. Call me old-fashioned, but a personality is also important.

I met Gosia at the popular General Merchants coffee shop in East Belfast. The menu would make London proud. Somewhere with world-class food, a choice of non-dairy milk and a varied menu that everyone raved about.

As a result, General Merchants was visited by celebrities, wannabe celebrities and the trendy people who had more money than most. Gosia sipped on her latte and I had a soy flat white.

She had a messy shag haircut that looked effortless. She was younger than I'd expected. Roughly late thirties, oversized sunglasses on her head, large earrings and a fake Gucci bag.

We did the European thing of kissing on each cheek. It was wonderful to meet someone who wasn't born and brought up in Northern Ireland. She had a different outlook on life and had travelled. Being foreign, I know Gosia would have experienced racism from many of the ignorant uneducated living in Ulster, so at least we had that in common, along with being business owners and living the single lifestyle.

"Cześć, dzień dobry, Gosia?" I said. This translated as, "Hello, how are you, Gosia?" in Polish. Gosia's face lit up. When I ran shipping conferences around the world, I learned basic phrases in over twenty languages, which helped me secure a lot of international business, including in the port of Gdansk in Poland.

"Terri told me you wouldn't disappoint," Gosia replied in her soft Polish accent.

"I like to stand out. You can expect a unique date from me. So what do you do for a living and why are you single?"

We both laughed. I'd asked the two worst questions you could ask at the beginning of a date.

Gosia told me she'd arrived in the UK only two years previously. She'd worked for minimum wage as a cleaner, yet believed she could do better. She worked six days a week and took business classes online in the evening while juggling two kids. Now she ran three successful cleaning companies in Belfast.

"So what brings you to Belfast?" I asked, impressed.

"Retail therapy with my mother. Matka, this is Niraj," she said. Matka means mother in Polish.

The woman beside her was in her late fifties, elegant, poised and reading a novel. Not looking at her phone, reading a book; how I miss seeing that. I didn't register her presence when I sat down, since she was at the adjacent table. I was once told if you want to know what a woman will look like when she gets older, check out her mother. This looked promising.

"Miło mi cię poznać," I said, which means, "Nice to meet you."

She lowered her book, gave a welcoming smile and replied back in perfectly pronounced Polish. While I can speak basic phrases in most languages I can't understand a word of it, so stupidly replied "awesome".

"Can we have some privacy?" I suggested to Gosia.

"I trust Matka's opinion. I need to be here legally."

"Why? How old are you?" I asked cautiously.

"I'm her legal guardian," Gosia explained.

"That's a relief! And well done on skipping the age question."

"A lady never reveals," she said. "So why is a charming man like you on Match?"

"You think I'm charming. Do you hear that, Matka?" A strange thing happened. Matka was no longer reading her book. She was studying me, like she was seeing if I was good enough for her daughter.

If my daughter was meeting a guy online, I'd probably do the same thing.

"Whereabouts do you live, Gosia?"

"Antrim."

"Why Antrim?"

"It has the biggest Polish population in Northern Ireland."

"Do you spend much time with Antrim people?"

"They don't care much for us. They don't care much for anyone. Protestant housing estates. Catholic housing estates. Nobody talks to the blacks or the Asians. This country is so far behind the rest of the modern world."

I know how she feels.

"Stay still," I said. I gently removed an eyelash from her cheek. "Now blow me and make a wish!"

Gosia jaw dropped as we both realised what I'd said.

"Sorry, oh God, no … I mean blow *it* and make a wish."

She could tell I was genuinely embarrassed.

"I need to keep an eye on you, Niraj."

"I'm so glad you can't see me go red."

Gosia was wonderful. Then again, so were many of the women I met and things hadn't worked out. So how do I bring this up subtly?

"I met a woman recently and thought she was amazing and she gave me the wrong phone number." Yes that was me being subtle and, now I hear it out loud, rather whiny.

"I met a man recently and thought he was amazing and

he stole my credit card and spent thousands of pounds on flatscreen TVs and iPads."

"Sorry, mine is worse."

Gosia let out a warm laugh. "Unlock your mobile," she said.

I did as I was told and handed it to her. She typed in a number and hit the green button. A *Star Wars* mobile ringtone went off. She removed the phone from her bag to reveal my number.

Our eyes locked and we just got each other.

"So glad you like *Star Wars*," I said relieved.

"If you don't like *Star Wars* or pineapple on pizza, we can't be together. What's your standards?

"Cream then jam, or jam then cream on scones?" I've actually seen people lose friendships over this.

"Always cream, then jam," said Gosia as if it were common sense.

"Same."

Gosia is a remarkable woman. We have so much in common. I can't think of one reason why this wouldn't work out.

Matka nudged her. "I'm going to check on her croissant, they were warming it up," Gosia said, getting up. She approached the counter, stepped back, kissed me on the cheek, then went back to the counter.

Wow. She was the real deal. Gosia could be the one. It had been one year yet it felt like ten years since I'd been with anyone. She was independent, smart, funny … and that smile! Wow! That's the kind of smile I want to wake up to every day.

I jumped up from my seat. Something was crawling up my leg. *What the hell?* I patted myself down. On second thoughts, it wasn't an insect, it was a foot, in a shoe. A woman's shoe.

I glanced over at Matka. She spoke in heavily accented English. “I like chubby coloured men.”

“Are you insane?”

“Sorry, I like vertically challenged men of colour. Is that okay, Mr Pee Wee?”

“It’s PC and your daughter is on a date with me!”

“She’s young, she doesn’t know what she wants. If she met a scarecrow in a field, she’d ask him out. Now me, I know how to please a man.”

I jumped up again as her foot edged higher, into areas it had no right to be edging towards.

“You and I will never be. Ever. Gosia is the only one I want,” I reminded her.

Gosia arrived with a croissant. She cut it in half and added jam. Matka sniffled.

“What’s wrong?” Gosia asked her.

Matka whispered in her ear. Gosia’s smile disappeared like she had been betrayed.

“Is this true, Niraj?”

I hesitated. *Would she really choose me over her mother?* “I’m afraid it is. The truth has to come out.”

Gosia threw her latte in my face. It was not burning hot, but enough to make me recoil. “You collect Hitler memorabilia!” she yelled.

By now everyone in the coffee shop was staring at us. I was baffled. *What the, what? How did …?*

“Do you know how difficult it is to come to this country as a foreigner?”

“Hello!” I gasped, pointing at my coloured face and every part of my body.

"You know what I mean! I'm foreign and I'm Polish and a cleaner. I put the U in underclass and it turns out you love the Third Reich!"

"Could you shout a bit louder?" I don't know why I said that. I should have just left.

"Yes! Yes, I can shout louder!" Gosia said, turning to the shop's other patrons. Then she turned back to me. "Call me when hell freezes over. I'll buy a defrosting machine and let you join Adolf."

Gosia stormed out, pulling Matka with her. Everyone gave me the dirtiest, nastiest looks.

As Gosia dragged her out, Matka mimed holding a phone, *Call me!*

Business Lesson Learned

There's often more than one person involved in the decision-making process. Depending on the size of the company, there can be up to several influencers and usually one final decision-maker. Gosia was the influencer, her mother was the decision-maker.

In business, how do you find out the people involved in the decision?

Never ask, "Are you the decision-maker?" The person always says yes, so you don't bother their boss. Frame it like this: "From my experience of dealing with companies like yours, there's often more than one person involved in the decision-making process. Who else do we have to speak to?"

This sets their mind at ease and makes them believe you won't go behind their back and call the boss.

"From my experience of dealing with companies like yours." That shows you're professional and have done this many times before.

"Who else do we have to speak to?" It means you see business as a partnership, which it is.

Chapter 16

CHARITY WORK

I needed a break from women.

That's a phrase I say a lot when expressing my frustration with online dating. "Why me?" and "Don't you love me, God" are the most common ones.

When I made my first donation to charity, it was £21 to Children in Need, a charity I knew from the annual TV fundraisers. It felt good. Like my soul had warmed up. Like I had done something meaningful and life had a bit more purpose. Then I did £21 a week later to the Samaritans, who help people that are depressed and suicidal, then a week later to Save the Children. It wasn't just a great thing to do, it fulfilled me and gave my life more meaning.

So I started giving twice a week and the donations increased to £31 per charity.

The more money I earned, the more I gave to charity. Running my own business years later meant my salary had plunged by fifty per cent, there was no benefit, no pension, nothing. While I still gave ten per cent of everything I earned after tax, it wasn't much, so I wanted to think of other ways to give.

I helped out Ride High MK, an equestrian centre which donated profits to helping disadvantaged children get therapy from horses. Since lockdown, the centre had been shut, so I delivered LinkedIn training and presentation skills to help the staff who were working tirelessly to raise funds during tough times. https://www.ridehigh.org/

Henry Allen Trust is a charity set up by the remarkable Dawn Allen, after losing her beloved son, Henry, to cancer. He was diagnosed with neuroblastoma at the age of two. As a parent, I can't imagine the horror of losing a child. I purchased colouring books, crayons, kids' playsets, Easter eggs, anything I could to make whatever time dying children had in the hospital more complete. https://thehenryallentrust.org.uk/

Two amazing friends run MK Charities. They give back to the community by running social media campaigns, helping unknown charities and those that are struggling. I mentored the co-founder on mindset, being happier with yourself and remaining calm under pressure and yes I'm aware of the irony. https://www.mkcharities.com/

It wasn't enough.

Then one day I did something I never thought I would do.

I gave away my possessions.

Dining table. Chairs. Microwave. Hoover. Flatscreen TV. Cupboards. Saucepans. Cutlery. Mugs and many things I didn't know I had.

Everything except 300 books on sales and personal development and my 1980s rock-music collection, from a limited edition *Karate Kid* soundtrack to *Born in the USA* by Bruce

Springsteen bought on the day of release. These would be coming back to Northern Ireland.

I was wasting so much money in storage over the last year and was wondering what I should do. So I spoke to my parents for advice.

"Give it to charity" was their simple answer.

There were a few things like a beautiful sofa with no fire sticker and a mattress that I had to throw away, unfortunately.

Everything else has been given away and will be sold for an amazing cause: Willen Hospice,who care for end-of-life patients and their families in Milton Keynes. https://www.willen-hospice.org.uk/

My suits, clothes, 200 fiction books, DVD player, DVDs including special edition *The Godfather*, *Back to the Future* and *Die Hard* box sets all went to Barnardos in Milton Keynes, who protect, support and nurture the UK's most vulnerable children. https://www.barnardos.org.uk/

What if I have to buy more sofas?

What if I have to buy beds?

What if I need extra cash?

I don't need loads of possessions to be happy in life. I need healthy parents, close friends, wonderful LinkedIn connections, awesome coaching clients, good mental health and a desire to serve others.

That's what matters most to me.

Money is important of course, although it's not the most important thing and it doesn't give you eternal happiness. How I wish I knew this decades ago, my life would be so much better.

I talked about this on social media because I wanted to

encourage others to give away more money or time to important causes.

That set social media on fire and made my personal brand stronger.

The post read like this:

Making the World a Better Place

On my fortieth birthday, my wife gave me a beautiful, limited-edition watch. I've always dreamed of an OMEGA since I'm a James Bond fan.

I tried it on, along with the Breitling; however, the sophistication and feel of the TAG Heuer won me over.

👍 I felt important.
👍👍 I felt powerful.
👍👍👍 I felt like I mattered.

✘ Unfortunately, I had to sell the watch in 2019 to help pay for the divorce.

My business then struggled in lockdown when my clients disappeared. It took me an unbearable year to rebuild. Since then, I've had twelve months of profit, paid off my loans and wanted to treat myself.

So I went to the jewellers yesterday to get a new TAG watch.

I tried on all the most expensive watches to make a purchase.

Something didn't feel right.

I'm a different person now than ten years ago.

I'm a different person now than a few years ago.

My whole world has changed and I see it differently.

If you think an expensive watch or sports car will make you happy, you have bigger problems in life.

So I gave the money to charity instead.

A table for ten people at the SportsAid charity event in Milton Keynes on 8th April. (I gave away the tickets to local charities.)

A table at the Milton Keynes Hospital Charity Ball on 24th June.

Sponsorship of several friends who are fundraising for good causes.

♥ If you want happiness, give to others.

End of post.

I had charities contacting me to support them for free. I had more people want to do business with me. After all, people want to work with people they like and trust. I picked up about 2,000 new followers on LinkedIn. Of all the social media platforms, this one mattered the most.

My mind was racing at this unexpected reaction. You want to help a few people and hundreds reach out. I went to Belfast to work at Grand Central Hotel, my favourite place for coffee in Belfast, a lush modern-day hotel with stunning views from the top floor. I treated myself to their chocolate sundae, which is heaven, and after replying to all the business enquiries, went for a walk to Tesco Express to get a smoothie.

Outside was Maeve, lots of kohl, early forties and short red hair. She held a charity box, collecting money for the environment.

My daughter is doing a degree in sustainability. She had

the choice of Oxford University, but chose Warwick University since they had an exchange programme with Australia.

"How much money would help?" I asked.

"How much do you have?" replied Maeve.

I reached into my wallet to give her a £5 note, except it wasn't a £5 note.

"Your business card. Bestselling author. Does that line work on women?"

"No sorry," I apologised. I fumbled for money in my wallet, "I meant to give you money."

"Sure you did," smiled Maeve.

I fumbled inside my wallet and gave her a £5 note.

"You win the lottery?" asked Maeve.

A long pause followed.

"Just trying to make the world right," I said, sort of awkwardly.

"Lots of sins," Maeve's right eyebrow arched.

"Yeah …"

"Were they illegal?" she enquired, her eyebrow still arched.

"No," I replied quickly.

"Then it's no big deal. It's part of life. You should come to my place of worship."

I gave her a cheeky smile, "Are you coming on to me?"

"Noooo."

"Your eyes say you like curry and your mouth says you like chocolate. You are coming on to me."

"I have a boyfriend."

"How original."

"You think you can impress women?"

"I know I can." Had no idea where this confidence came from, but I was enjoying the repartee.

"How about you show me what you can do on Sat. night ...?"

She looked at me; I couldn't tell if she liked me or wanted to punch me.

"Meet me 7 p.m. tonight at The Tipsy Bird. Dress smart. Ask for Maeve."

"Do you own the bar?"

"All will be revealed." She gave me a naughty smile and I returned to the car park, only to realise I forgot to buy a bottle of water.

Business Lesson Learned

Giving makes the world a better place.

It's brings attention to issues many people didn't know about.

It's wonderful for your confidence and inner worth.

The more you give, the more you get back.

It's good for your reputation, you feel like you belong and you even save on tax relief.

Giving sets an excellent example for future generations.

"No one has ever become poor from giving." – Anne Frank

Chapter 17

NETWORKING

Every time I go on a date I'm nervous. I want it to go right. Also, people don't realise how exhausting it is to work as a coach all day listening to people – then spend your evenings with online dating trying to listen attentively.

If there was a way to skip from the first date to date seven, that would interest me.

I arrived at The Tipsy Bird in central Belfast. It's a modern-day pub with a classic pub feel to it. It was half empty, typical of most bars during the week. People don't venture out that much to pubs anymore unless it's summer, 2 for 1 drinks or there's a big sporting event on.

Lots of men sat alone. One wore a tracksuit top; the rest all wore shirts and trousers. The women made a huge effort. They were drinking cocktails, laughing and chatting away.

I purchased special insoles from Amazon that I tucked into my polished black shoes. It made me two inches higher and I had to work my core hard when I talked. It gave me a swagger that I liked. Went to Cloak and Dagger beforehand for a Turkish shave and I scrubbed up well.

Maeve had a flower in her hair and welcomed me with a lovely smile. I reached out to shake her hand. A taller man with a beard interrupted with his handshake. "I'm Maeve's boyfriend. We've been awaiting you."

What have I got myself into?

"Help yourself to a drink, we start in five minutes. Ladies, this is Niraj, he's here for the dating event."

Before I could reply with "say what now?" I was welcomed by the single ladies. Ten of them all staring at me and smiling. I had no idea what to say.

"Where are you from?" asked Lisa, a short woman with glasses and spikey hair.

"Northern Ireland."

"Me too. Let's get married," joked Lisa and all the women laughed out loud.

"What kind of speed dating is this?" I asked curiously.

"Speed dating makes me nervous," replied Lisa. "It's more of a singles evening where we mingle and talk to each other."

Except the men weren't mingling or talking to anyone. They stared at their mobiles, flicking through the Sky Sports app and maybe dating websites for all I knew.

I have spent years attending business networking events and I knew how to make them work. "So what do you want to achieve tonight?"

They all started talking over each other, with energy and excitement. It was fun.

"A nice guy." "A decent fella." "Someone I can have a laugh with, so I do." "Speak for yourself, I just want to get shagged," blurted Lisa causing more raucous laughter.

"Okay, I will keep an eye out for you all," I reassured them.

"What are you looking for, Niraj?" asked Lisa.

That's a good question. Nobody had ever asked me that. "I don't know … but I'll know when I meet her."

Fionnuala, a tall, curvy beauty therapist arrived with a glass of white wine in her hand. "What did I miss?"

"Just found your dream man, Fionnuala," said Lisa. "He's a pervert just like you."

Before I could object, the women laughed. They were here to have fun.

I went over and talked to the guys. I asked their names, what they did and what kind of woman they wanted. I typed furiously on my phone. Responses varied from "I want someone who isn't a psycho", "A woman of faith" to "Someone I can have sparks with". And what skills do you have? Answers varied from "DIY" to "gardening" to "cricket".

This was so different to speed dating in Soho where everyone was tense and awkward. This was going to be light-hearted and I liked Fionnuala. There was something about her.

I was here to have fun, not find the perfect woman, although if we hit it off and went out, I wouldn't complain.

"Good luck, Fionnuala, I hope you don't meet anyone you like," I said and winked at her.

She smiled back at me and her smile lit up the room.

I sat opposite a large, friendly woman in her fifties. "How can I help you?"

"I'd like to meet someone who, you know, maybe likes walks along the beaches and shares my faith."

"I know just the guy for you. Over there, Dave, you will love him. Come on over." The lady accompanied me. "Dave, this is my good friend …" I didn't know her name.

"Gail," she interrupted and sat down beside Dave. "What's your faith?"

"Christian," he replied shyly.

"Me too," said Gail.

I let them be and went over to the next lady. "Who are you looking for?" I asked Carolyn, a petite blonde with curly hair.

"A rich man who can do DIY."

I checked my phone. "Come and meet Barry." I introduced them.

Next up was April, half black, half Irish, absolutely stunning, posh English accent. We got on like a house on fire. We had so much in common although I had my sights set on Fionnuala.

"Someone who likes the sea and can spend a day watching cricket."

I checked my phone to remind myself of who was interested in what and introduced her to Colly, who mentioned his love of cricket.

One by one, I worked the room, just like I do at business events, asking lots of questions and matching people up with potential clients. In this case, potential mates.

I sat down exhausted at the end of the evening, feeling good. People were nice to me. I felt wanted. Like I mattered. I was a different person.

Fionnuala sat beside me. She spoke her mind and played with her hair while she talked to me. "I like how you work the room."

"I have other skills too."

"Not just a pretty face," she added.

"How many drinks have you had?" I enquired.

"Still on the first one. I like to keep my mind clear."

"Who do you want to meet tonight?" I asked.

She turned around to check nobody could hear her, like she was letting me in on a secret. "An Indian man with no hair and a unique accent."

"There's about 500 million of those. Be more specific?" I smiled.

She handed me her business card. "This is to prove to you I'm not insane. You can find my footprint on Google."

I read her card and couldn't wait to find out more.

"I want someone with a handkerchief in their top pocket. A sharp white shirt and brown shoes. He knows how to wash and wears aftershave that attracts rather than overwhelms." Fionnuala knew how to read my mind. She made eye contact and chose her words carefully. "Someone who knows how to dance."

I moved close to her, our lips within kissing distance. "Dancing is my middle name."

When you attend weddings and see dads hitting the dance floor, uncoordinated, out of sync and everyone laughing at their terrible moves, that is me – and I wasn't going to let that ruin an opportunity with a woman who was sober, sexy, smart, liked me and had no baggage.

I didn't even wait till I got home. I rushed to the car park, looked up her name. Successful business. Amicable divorce? Could I finally have found true love?

Business Lesson Learned

If you're an introvert and you're nervous about networking, don't worry, most people are nervous to network. Introverts do well at networking events because they ask questions and listen. You don't have to be a smooth operator to win the room.

The worst thing you can say as soon as you meet someone at a networking event is "What do you do?" It's unoriginal and doesn't make you memorable.

Mention your name and ask "What brings you here?" When you've listened to their answer, ask "So, who do you want to meet tonight?"

Introduce them to their ideal customer.

If you don't know who the ideal customer is, ask the event organiser. They want everything to go smoothly, it's good for their reputation.

Networking is similar to sales. It's not about getting what you want. It's helping others get what they want. That's smart for your personal brand, and karma/the law of attraction/kismet/fate, call it what you like, kicks into action.

Chapter 18

UNDERSTAND THE COMPETITION

Priyanka loved to dance. At weddings, she owned the dance floor with her moves. She had presence, like a movie star from the 1950s. Like Grace Kelly – stylish, beautiful, yet she had a sharp tongue that could tear you to pieces if you got on the wrong side of her.

For years she'd asked me to go salsa dancing and I'd always had excuses:

"I've had a long day at work." "Football is on tonight. Liverpool are going to win the Premier League, I can feel it." They only won once in twenty-one years.

Sometimes I even ate in McDonald's on my way home from work in London, just so I could walk into the house late, mumbling, "Sorry, missed dance class again." I always chewed two sticks of gum, to hide the burger smell, and would squirt aftershave all over myself before I entered the house, but Priyanka knew. She always knew. She was a dignified wife who'd put up with too much disappointment from me.

I wasn't going to make the same mistake with Fionnuala.

This time, no matter what, I was going to make this relationship work. Having spent a few days watching beginner's salsa videos on YouTube, I was still terrified. In the movies, they make it look sexy and cool. In real life, it was complicated with intricate feet movement AND eye contact AND balance AND you have to smile or at least be suave.

This was too risky. Then I came across bachata, a Dominican Republic dance that was slower and much easier with music inspired by African beats.

I went onto Google and found a bachata dance class in East Belfast which showed the inside of the hall full of happy people dancing. When I turned up, it was high-gated, covered in barbed wire and had CCTV, like you were entering prison rather than attending a dance class. No wonder they didn't show the outside.

I offered to pick up Fionnuala; however, she was independent and met me there instead. We arrived together. Fionnuala wore a summer dress with white trainers for easy movements. Being clueless, I wore my same smart outfit from the dating events, simply swapped my shirt and replaced shoes with trainers. Why stray too far from a look that works?

"You know how to show a woman a good time?" said Fionnuala, a mixture of fun and sarcasm.

"Wait till you have the McDonald's special I have lined up afterwards," I replied.

I prepared to walk inside. Fionnuala grabbed my hand. "I want to make sure there's no tension between us tonight. I don't play games and I make quick decisions."

"Where was this going?"

"At my age, nobody has time to waste."

I know you shouldn't ask a woman her age, but now all I wanted to do was ask her age.

Before I could reply, she planted her lips on mine. It was passionate and I pulled her body close, enjoying every moment.

"Good. Now we can dance," smiled Fionnuala.

The dance class consisted of nine people: four men and five women. They were all younger and skinnier than me – story of my life. The hall was a studio gym. The medicine balls, weights, skipping ropes and large balancing balls were all tucked into the corner. A half-empty water dispenser stood to one side.

The salsa instructor made his entrance in front of the tall, mirrored studio wall and I did a double-take. He was Indian, 5 foot 8 inches, bald, had an accent that wasn't English and wore a tank top.

"Ladies and gentlemen," said the Indian salsa instructor with a strong Ballycastle accent, sort of a countryside Northern Irish accent. "My name is Nilash."

"Is that your …?"

"No, it's not my brother," I quickly reacted to Fionnuala, although the similarities were scary.

"We're going to get warmed up," Nilash said. He played a Latino song on his iPhone: trumpets, bongo, maracas, tambourine and piano.

"Move your shoulders back and forth six times!" I did as I was told. So far, so good.

"Now lean forward, give your left leg a good stretch and repeat with your right leg." That was a bit tougher with my osteoarthritis, but I managed it. I glanced over to Fionnuala, who moved effortlessly.

"Now swing your arms around your head. Continuing to ten, nine, eight ..."

We swung our arms. I stopped. My face froze. Nothing worse than running into your ex in public.

Sarah was there. The one who'd slept with me, recorded us together to get her boyfriend back and stood me up at the restaurant. She wore a top that left little to the imagination, not that I was imagining anything. She caught my eye in the mirror then ignored me. I want nothing to do with her, at the same time I don't want to be ignored. What was she doing in Belfast?

"Okay, now get into your couples and let's begin. Men, centre your feet, take a small step forward with your left foot. Raise your hands slightly, we're not robots. Ladies, as the men step forward on the left, you step back on the right foot. Relax your hips then ladies, step forward on your right and men step back on your left. Let's practise."

The four women stood opposite with their four male partners. Sarah was left alone until Nilash approached her. "I will dance with my wife."

"Nooo ..." I said, louder than I should have.

"What's wrong?" asked Fionnuala.

"We have to win this competition," I insisted.

"It's beginner's bachata."

"We're going to win and you're going to post this everywhere. Not just Facebook. I want it on Myspace, AOL and Yahoo."

"AOL? Awesome sauce, Grandad?" joked Fionnuala.

"Sarah's my ex. She had sex and never spoke to me again."

"You just described every man's dream come true," replied Fionnuala confused.

"The enemy deserves no mercy," I said, quoting one of the greatest movies of all time, *Karate Kid*.

"Five, six, seven, eight ..." uttered Nilash with more flare than was necessary.

Everyone danced in unison, or as close to unison as you can in a beginner's class. Fionnuala and I danced towards Nilash and Sarah.

"One more time ... Five, six, seven, errrrr ..."

On eight, I bumped into Sarah, causing her to lose balance and almost fall over.

"Oopsy. First time!" I replied, with a hint of wickedness.

Nilash and Sarah got their balance back. Sarah whispered in his ear. Nilash growled. This was not going to have a happy ending.

Nilash sounded hysterical. "No matter what happens, no matter what you witness, keep dancing until I say stop. And five, six, seven, eight ..."

Nilash and Sarah danced aggressively towards us. Fionnuala and I danced away, then sideways, zig-zagging across the studio trying to get away from Sarah and Nilash.

For the first time, I saw Fionnuala move away.

"We have a mission to accomplish," I reminded her.

"This is not what I came here for," she reminded me. "Take revenge in your own time."

Before we could reply, Sarah grabbed the large balancing ball and threw it at Fionnuala, knocking her over.

Everyone stopped dancing. "Keep dancing!" Nilash yelled at everyone. The worried beginners kept moving awkwardly, trying to comprehend what was going on while two bald Indian men set examples of how adults should never behave.

Fionnuala grabbed a heavy medicine ball and marched like a juggernaut towards Sarah. I stood in the way.

"I'm a respected coach, I can't let you do that," I insisted.

After careful consideration, Fionnuala agreed. "You're right."

"Take your fat ass and get out of my class!" demanded Nilash to Fionnuala.

Fionnuala threw the ball at Nilash's left foot. He screamed in pain while hopping around on his other foot.

I should have punched him in the face; however, I don't believe in violence. So I slapped him, reluctantly. Dumbfounded, he slapped me back, quite gently. Offended, I slapped ever so slightly harder. Frustrated, Nilash went to kick me with his right foot. I caught it and lifted his right leg higher, stretching it. "How does that feel, Osama bin Laden?"

I've no idea why I called him that, he was Indian.

Sarah grabbed a skipping rope and wrapped it around Fionnuala's neck and Sarah choked her from behind. Fionnuala wriggled, but Sarah was too strong.

By now the class had escaped, like monsters were loose.

I pushed Nilash's stretched right leg as hard as I could and heard a crack. It wasn't his trousers ripping, it was a muscle. He fell over hard. I went to help Fionnuala. "Get your hands off my girlfriend!" I said to Sarah. I tried to undo the rope from her neck, but Sarah was pulling too tight. Fionnuala struggled to breathe. "Punch her!" she gasped.

"I'm not hitting another woman." So I stuck my leg out. Fionnuala pushed and Sarah fell over. Then Fionnuala pushed over the half-empty water dispenser, which toppled over and landed on Sarah with a powerful thud.

A & E is never a nice place to queue. Due to social distancing, there was a long wait outside. Drunks, drug addicts, people bloodied from fights and people with colds and flu. That's the problem with the NHS. When you have a free service, many people will take advantage. You don't need A & E for a cold – and yes, I'm aware of the irony of going to A & E after being in a jealous fight with an ex who rejected me.

Rope burns had formed around Fionnuala's neck. I reached over to kiss her and she moved away.

"Do you know what I do," asked Fionnuala on a serious note.

"Of course. An awesome jewellery business and a degree in history. Impressive."

She stared into the distance, avoiding eye contact. "Abraham Lincoln was my favourite of all time. He had to endure so much failure in his life and he maintained his integrity despite life's setbacks."

"You think I'm Lincoln?"

"I hoped you were. Turns out you're a John Wilkes Booth."

"I'm not a murderer," I protested.

"More a metaphorical one. Booth thought that by harming Lincoln he was doing the greater good. All he did was destroy his legacy and hurt a great president. Most men have egos and I'm not at a point in my life where I want to deal with them."

She got up to leave. "I'm sorry, please don't go," I begged her.

Her mind was made up. A painful lesson learned.

Business Lesson Learned

So often, things seem fine. Then boom, something gets in your way that throws you off balance. It's usually a competitor. They can be unknown, or someone you've known for years.

Never criticise the competition, it makes you look bad. When they take the low road, you take the high road. The more you attack them, the weaker you become. Say nothing. Even better, say nice things about them. That will surprise your client and make you look good.

Recently, I've begun working with my competitors: speaking at their events, talking to the people in their membership programme, talking on their podcasts. It's been mutually beneficial, in terms of relationships and money.

"Before you embark on a journey of revenge, dig two graves." – Confucius

Chapter 19

STOICISM

I'd not seen my daughter in a while and, when I call, conversation is always stilted. It's hard to build a relationship on a phone without hugs or being in the presence of someone.

Lockdown had been fully lifted and people were slowly starting to travel.

My business was making money and with working twelve hours a day and trying to meet the right person with online dating for one to two hours a night, I needed time to think, time to smile and time to catch up with old friends.

During my divorce, I realised the people I thought were my closest friends weren't. They were simply people that I knew.

I was now doing business with people that I'd only met over Zoom. I wanted to spend time with Freya, especially with her twenty-first birthday coming up, which I was going to celebrate. I'd also built up amazing relationships very quickly thanks to my explosive growth on LinkedIn.

One of the most important things you can do on LinkedIn is stand out and be different. I've not seen anyone tour the

UK to meet clients, so thought, why not me? That way I can combine all three joys.

I spent five days planning a two-week trip. A few people were on holiday, everybody else was happy to meet me, which I was honoured by. I am not a fan of driving, especially around the South of England with the M1, M25 and roadworks causing long delays; however, that was the easiest option.

I took an overnight ferry to Liverpool and first stop was Leicestershire to meet the following people. If you're on LinkedIn, connect with these people below and learn from them, they are amazing.

Adam Fox. I pitched sales training to Adam's company years ago and they were already working with somebody else. Most people give up and move on. This is a big mistake businesses make. "No" often means not right now. You need to build trust and develop the relationship.

I got on great with Adam, supported his charity work and treated him well. When he left to set up his business, who did he contact? Me.

Next up in Stoke was my client Anna Wooliscroft, a copywriter. Copy-writing is one of the most underrated skills in business and it was such an honour to meet Anna and get taken out for a lovely breakfast.

I was due to have dinner with Freya. Unfortunately, some kid was driving his father's car too fast and ran me off the road. My car was badly damaged and I missed dinner with my daughter. Instead, I had to get help, sort insurance and get a replacement car.

The next day, I cancelled all meetings, still dealing with car insurance and replacements and quite shook up from the car crash. In the evening, I had a charity dinner. I thought it would be wonderful for Freya to meet many of the amazing women running the charities in Milton Keynes. It's vital a child, especially a daughter, knows there are no limitations on success. That there are amazing women everywhere in important positions who can make a difference. She met Ride High MK and MK Charities, who were excellent role models; the other charities unfortunately cancelled last moment.

Next was the fabulous Debbie Lewis of NatWest who gave me my first big speaking gig, followed by wonderful Laura Chapman, communications manager at McDonald's. They bid for my coaching services at a Ronald McDonald House fundraiser and, after many cancellations, I finally had the opportunity to work with them.

My brilliant estate agent Alex Carvello of The Right Place followed. He took care of my house while I was away and rented it out, ensuring I had extra income after my mortgage was taken care of, to pay for this holiday: hotels, gifts, food and drink and petrol.

Nick Raeburn is an epic video expert in Bournemouth. Took me three hours getting to his house. We had a ball talking business while bonding with his adorable kids and walking in the glorious summer sunshine, then another two hours' drive to meet the king of social selling, Daniel Disney. When I needed LinkedIn advice, Daniel was the first person I invested in and it's one of the best investments I ever made.

Five hours later, I ended up in Devon; that was a long trip. Lots of lovely English countryside to meet the power duo Laura

Tejada and Louise Ansell. Laura was the one who helped me with my dating profile and supported me loads in lockdown.

Clare Carroll is a brilliant content creator I met on LinkedIn. She was nearby in Devon and we had lunch outside the stunning Exeter Cathedral. Despite only knowing Clare for a few months, I felt like I'd known her for years – that's how easy she is to get on with.

The journey to west London took almost eight hours in a car; I could have flown to India in less time. Traffic was brutal on the back roads.

Alex Alleyne is one the top sales directors in the UK. Met him in Canary Wharf, east London and we geeked out on sales. After that was fellow Salesforce Influencer Galem Girmay, who made me lovely apple crumble at her flat where I also hung out with her adorable dog, Poppy; and then Steve Burton, a funny northerner who is also a master networker and someone I regularly turn to for advice.

Sunday I drove to north of London and went from north-west to north-east London to meet Suzette Coon, a brilliant playwright who I worked with many decades ago; Ben Pessok, one of my first clients in the 1990s, who spends his days in retirement making the world better doing charity work; and James Epstein, a brilliant sales manager who I worked with years ago and one of the funniest people I knew.

Driving so far to meet these people sounds excessive. If you want relationships to work in business, you need to put in the effort. You can't hope for others to do it first or wait around for things to happen. Action cures many things.

Mike Ashton, former marketing director of Hilton Hotels

UK, hired me for coaching work in lockdown, so I took him out for a thank-you lunch. He's also a drummer in the best Beatles cover band, The Dung Beatles, so that was a fun chat.

I could feel my arteries clogging from the rich food and time spent driving, so I changed location and met Dawn Clark at Willen Hospice for a countryside stroll where we talked charity work and making the world better.

Yumchop Foods make food with an African twist. The flavours are superb and they're expanding beyond universities into the business world. Abi Adefisan and her husband Michael run a fast-growing business and I took their entire family out to thank them for being a client.

Mark Walker, former army officer, runs facilities management and security business Ashridge Group. Mark is my client and he welcomed me to his offices like a long-lost friend. We had coffee and croissants and lots of lovely cake.

Rina Singh owns a Resilience Pod podcast. I was honoured to be a guest and it's one of my most valuable interviews. We had coffee and croissants and lots of lovely cake. I'm seeing a theme here.

Amanda Rowe is the hypnotherapist I go to when I need help. She's brilliant and a lovely human being. Had a delicious pub dinner with Amanda and her new partner.

I packed a LOT into this trip. Business is relationships. With many people I brought a book I thought they would enjoy reading. I shared insight that I thought would help their business. I gave advice on improving their LinkedIn profile. It's all about giving; that's what good business is.

Ranjit Singh, of Milton Keynes Community Foundation,

helps businesses, charities and philanthropists do the right kind of giving.

Craig Langley, who I met on audio-only app Clubhouse, that started with a bang and continued with a whimper, is a legend in automation.

Precious Zumbika-Lwanga is a force of nature, business strategist, woman in construction and board advisor who I know through Ranjit. I can't reveal what we talked about but it was legendary.

I'm not comfortable taking photos because I never look good in them. Then I hired David Wellbelove, who spent two hours working with me and doing photos for my dating profile and business profile. The first photos I've ever had done that I thought were great.

AJ Yates is a mental health expert with a wicked sense of humour who looks like Jack Dee (his words not mine) and someone I worked with. We talked mental health over delicious Indian food.

Razi Afghan, the nicest person I know, has always supported me in my charity efforts; and Yasmin Ulhaq, founder and director of Glenfield Asset Management, is a luxury-property and lifestyle manager who I was lucky enough to coach.

Then a nine-hour round trip to Wales to meet relentlessly helpful nerd John Espirian. We talked Liverpool, parenthood, the joys of pineapple on pizza and John would later become my coach, taking me to another level.

For every meeting a picture went on social media. I stressed the importance of building relationships in a digital world. It's good for your image and how people perceive you.

I recommend this to everyone. It went smoothly, then it all fell apart.

Priyanka called me to say that when I arrived at the house to meet Freya, there would be another man there, someone she had been seeing for "some time". We're divorced, why should I care?

I cared because I'm suffering relentlessly in online dating and she clicks her fingers and men come running. I care because I lost so much in the divorce and it always feels like she's doing better.

I know you shouldn't compare, but with your ex-partners, you do compare, it's human nature.

This guy had been living with her for several months and she kept it a secret to make sure it had value. That's fine, except my daughter lives in the same home with this guy and I shouldn't have been kept out of the loop. As her father, I had a right to know.

Then she told me she moved Freya's twenty-first birthday till after I had left because it was convenient for her. That meant I would miss my daughter's special day.

My meeting with Freya was a disaster. When I picked her up at Priyanka's house, I met her new boyfriend. A tall, handsome silver fox. He seemed like a nice guy, but I felt inferior around him. My ex-wife had upgraded to a better model and I was still needing a major regular service.

It should have been an evening spent on bonding and listening to her. Instead, I was angry and hurt. I used language I shouldn't have used. We barely said a word. After dinner, I left Freya at home. She was livid that I was so involved in my own problems and not hers and told me that I needed to raise my standards, which, ironically, is what I say to my clients who need help.

The next day, I went to Waterstones in Milton Keynes and asked for books on stoicism. Stoicism has become popular recently thanks to Ryan Holiday's outstanding *The Daily Stoic*, which is like a Cliffs Notes for Shakespeare, making it accessible to the masses. I also purchased *Ego is the Enemy* by Ryan.

Stoicism is about finding meaning and purpose in life. Plato, Socrates, Marcus Aurelius, the greater philosophers of all time practised stoicism and they had a lot to teach us. It's about controlling our thoughts and doing the greater good. Sort of a mixture of EQ, mindset, delayed gratification and charity work.

So many people have success then throw it away with bad emotional decisions and ego. During my eight-hour ferry ride home from Liverpool to Belfast I studied these books in detail. Over the next month, I reread them, underlined, then took action. I would never let that mistake happen again.

I told Freya what I had done to improve. For an introvert, she knew how to lecture me. Then I saw her twenty-first birthday photos. Not of me. Only her friends, Priyanka and her new partner. That broke my heart. Imagine not being able to share happiness with your daughter on her birthday.

I'm out of sight. I'm out of touch. People don't think about you. A lot like business in many ways.

From then on, I swore things would change. I told Freya I would fly to England every two weeks to have dinner with her. She was shocked. Every two weeks! That way, she would see me regularly, not just now and again. You can't build a relationship now and again. Over the phone, you can go quiet. Over dinner, you have to make more effort at bonding.

It would cost me an extra £1,200 a month, approx. $1,600 a month. That's $2,000 a month extra I had to earn every month before taxes kick in.

I raised my prices twenty per cent and with all the social media pictures of me with clients and friends, I had more business enquiries and converted more business. Like I said, people buy people.

I picked up enough business to pay for flights, hotels and taxis back and forth from England to spend time with my daughter and still give her some extra cash for university.

She wouldn't celebrate any important event again without her father.

Business Lesson Learned

Stoicism is centuries old, yet the thinking is just as relevant and modern today.

My favourite stoic quotes are:

"The best answer to anger is silence." – Marcus Aurelius

"Let us prepare our minds as if we'd come to the end of our lives. Let us postpone nothing." – Marcus Aurelius

"When we are no longer able to change a situation, we are challenged to change ourselves." – Viktor Frankl

"The key is to keep company with only those that uplift you, whose presence calls forth your best." – Epictetus

"How does it help to make troubles heavier by bemoaning them." – Seneca

"Whenever there is a human being, we have an opportunity for kindness." – Seneca

Chapter 20

UNDERSTANDING SALES PROCESS

There's an old saying, "It's lonely at the top."

It's also lonely when you have nobody to share your life with. It's lonely when you spend Friday nights working, on top of your nine-to-five work. It's lonely when you get a takeaway and binge watch Netflix because there's nobody to share your life with.

I was travelling back and forth to England, travelling across the country to see clients, yet eating alone in restaurants. I often took my laptop for company. I found it strange that I was doing so well at work, had the respect of my peers, yet still felt something was missing. So I decided to try something new.

It's vital to keep evolving in business. If it doesn't work, it doesn't work, but at least make the effort. So many people give up too quickly and spend their lives complaining or blaming others. That was not going to be me. So I decided to treat dating like sales.

Sales is the foundation of your business. Without sales, your business doesn't exist.

People misunderstand sales as bad car salesmen or awful

call-centre staff mis-selling to you. Do these people exist? Absolutely. I've trained call-centre staff and most of them are good people. They're badly advised by their bosses. Most car salesmen are good people, again, some are very badly trained by narrow-minded bosses and terrible sales training companies who haven't evolved in the last thirty years.

Sales people are not the problem; their bosses are, for failing to understand sales, failing to move with the times and living with a "greed first, people second" philosophy.

It disappoints me with how we've changed as a society with lockdown – remote working, mental health awareness, Zoom, reliance on technology – that one of the world's oldest professions, selling, hasn't evolved much.

I knew sales. I made my living as a coach and mentor helping others succeed and generate more sales. I could do this and apply it to dating.

If you dive into sales with a desperation and a selfishness for your own needs, people can sense it a mile off.

I was a different person now. I hardly recognised myself from a few years ago when I battled depression and lost my business. I often wonder why I had to endure what I did. You learn through failure and heartache more than success. I wish you didn't learn that way. I wish you learned through happiness, although that's not how the world works.

Photographer David Wellbelove made me look good on camera, something nobody has ever achieved. I updated my profile on all dating websites. I talked about myself, but not too much. I included pictures of myself around the UK. When women did contact me, I didn't reply immediately, that's too desperate.

I read their profiles before we spoke, I talked about them, I asked questions: the basic building blocks of sales and business.

I listened. Listening is a superpower and a skill not many people have. Women are much better than men at listening.

I learned to be patient. Everyone rushes too quickly in sales and I've certainly been guilty of that.

Then and only then did I talk about myself. When I did, it was short, punchy sentences, not waffling about me, me, me, like most people.

I had fun. I didn't take myself too seriously. When they went quiet, I kept giving value, sharing a joke, asking the highlight of their day. Most people went quiet. Why? It doesn't always mean they're not interested. It means they're busy doing other things, sometimes urgent things. You have to be there. Be seen. On dating websites, I showed photos of me with friends, including other women. Social proof matters.

If I heard nothing, I tried again. Business is in the follow-up, you rarely win at the first attempt. So keep trying.

One night Orla contacted me through Match. Orla means golden princess in Gaelic, so that was a positive sign. She lived fifty miles away on the Northern Irish coast, several miles from the stunning Giant's Causeway. It was autumn, the weather was turning cold and I had no desire to make a two-hour round trip for a date that might go nowhere.

So I talked to more women, asked questions and had meetings. This time over drinks, not dinner. If there was no magic after thirty minutes, I explained it wasn't working and I wanted to save them time and save myself time; some appreciated it, some didn't. I got stood up a few more times and I didn't get depressed, because that's sales. I took a business book with me to all dates, so I would keep myself busy until they arrived instead of desperately waiting by looking up every few seconds.

Orla contacted me again a week later. She asked me questions and commented on my profile. In other words, she was being me. I liked that. So I agreed to meet on Zoom first.

She was the same age as me and had an easy-going manner about her. Orla wore a Rolling Stones T-shirt and we spent the entire time sharing our favourites tracks; "Sympathy for the Devil" was hers (the greatest lyrics to any song) and mine is "Out of Time", a mixture of rock and Motown. She had a candle in the background and so did I. We were speaking over each other as we talked about why our teenage daughters drive us mad.

Either this was someone I would spend the rest of my life with, or we would get on like a house on fire then get bored. Time would tell.

We agreed to meet at the Bushmills Inn, a luxurious pub and hotel near Orla's house. Cast members of *Game of Thrones* often stayed there. I emailed them beforehand to let them know I was on a date; staff went out of their way to make everything comfortable.

Many businesses have used Covid and Brexit as an excuse for shoddy customer services. Thankfully, Bushmills Inn was a cut above the others.

The fireplace sparked gently. The bar served several types of the famous Bushmills whiskey. Everyone was dressed in their finest clothes. The crowd was my age and older. Bushmills Inn is steeped in Irish history. Over 400 years old, this was warm and welcoming. Orla wore a long turquoise dress and smiled with warmth. Her eyes were kind, and when you hugged her, the world made more sense.

After drinks, we enjoyed a delicious meal and shared a sticky toffee pudding for dessert. She was as nervous as me, had been single many years and when she spoke about her enjoyment of *Married at First Sight* and cheesy reality shows, I nodded politely, clueless to what she was talking about.

"I didn't think you'd reply to me, Niraj. You must be popular with the ladies."

"I wish I could go back in time and tell the nerdy me in high school that it would be okay."

"It couldn't have been as bad as my NHS glasses," replied Orla.

"I had acne like my face was made of pizza."

Orla took out her mobile. "I've had all my old photos transferred." She showed me a picture of her younger, skinnier self, with geeky braids, thick glasses and brown school uniform. I showed a few pics of my younger, skinnier self with hair and a six-pack. Okay, it was my rock-star poses when I failed as a rock star aged nineteen.

"You look handsome." There was no sarcasm in her voice and she was only on her second glass of sweet rosé.

"Do you like chocolate?" I asked curiously.

"Of course I do," replied Orla.

"No, I mean chocolate men like me with brown skin." I know subtlety isn't my strong point, but I'm going to be fifty soon. I don't know how many good years I have left.

She covered her mouth like I had said something illegal.

"You can't say that, it's not politically correct."

"Do you …? I asked, hoping for the right answer.

"I happen to find Indian men attractive."

"Really? What is it? Our big noses? Our love handles? Our shortness in height?"

"Oh, no, I don't care about looks," said Orla casually.

"That's comforting," I replied.

"Indian men have strong family values. That matters to me, and your food – it's my favourite."

"Indian food in Northern Ireland is awful," I reminded her.

"I know," agreed Orla. "I've had it in Blackburn and Southall. A different world of tastes and flavours."

"So you're well-travelled?" I asked.

"As much as you can be as a single mum on a social worker's salary."

My family work in the NHS. I know the vital work social workers do, saving children from alcoholic fathers or mothers that shoot up heroin. Trying to calm down a hostile parent with no police protection. Like a lot of important people in this world, social workers don't get paid what they're worth.

"So you save lives, you're funny, you like Indian men."

"Impressed?" asked Orla.

"This is the part where I usually wake up and have my cornflakes," I replied.

Orla laughed, loudly. She had a fabulous laugh. Then she played with her hair while we spoke. I quite liked it. "I'm having a lovely evening with you."

I stared into her eyes with comfort. So was I. "What else are you looking for in a relationship?"

"We women want a man to keep us on our toes. We want a man who is loyal. We want a man who can do handiwork around the house, yet still have time for sex when we say it's okay. He has to love my family regardless of how they behave. We want a man who doesn't agree with everything we say, yet does everything we tell him to do."

"That makes no sense whatsoever," I said, flabbergasted.

"Welcome to modern-day dating," replied Orla. She took my hand. "I have good instincts about people. You're a good man who respects women."

Orla was right, although no woman had noticed that so far. "I have something I'd like to show you in the back seat of my car."

"Maybe I spoke too soon," said Orla.

"No, I promise, it will only take a few minutes."

"That's how my youngest was born."

"Let me explain. There's not much to do in Northern Ireland when you're single. I started attending food markets to taste new flavours and meet new people. I became friends with Gavin who runs the Little Popcorn Shop and he has put together some fresh homemade salted-caramel popcorn that will blow your mind into another dimension. Not that nonsense you get in the shops. I'm talking moreish, heart-pounding, make-me-thirsty-for-more popcorn."

"Why are you still here? Go!" urged Orla, eager for a taste.

I rushed to the front of the Bushmills Inn in the dark, grabbed the popcorn from the back seat, and dashed back to our table.

Orla was gone. Flustered, I approached the waitress. "The lady in the turquoise dress. Where did she go?"

"Sorry, sir. She left," said the waitress.

"Maybe she went to the bathroom," I said hopefully.

"I saw her go that-a-way," said the waitress, pointing to the car park.

Where did I go wrong? I checked my breath, my zip wasn't undone and my shirt wasn't hanging out. I didn't have her mobile so couldn't call her.

I went onto the Match app and she wasn't active. I rushed outside out the back door into the freezing cold. There was Orla, coming in from the car park, holding a cupcake for me. "My daughter makes the best cakes. Thought it would be nice to share dessert with you."

I held up the popcorn. "Great minds think alike."

First dates don't have to set the world on fire. Sometimes it can be as simple as being with someone you are comfortable with. Who makes you feel like you matter. Someone you can have a delicious dessert with.

Having a great first date is tough. Having a great second date is even tougher.

For our second date, we went to Galgorm Kitchen, four nights later.

In between, various women had finally started contacting me on Match. In business, you don't just speak to one client, you have to speak to a variety of people and have multiple meetings to see how you connect. To see who you want to work with – and also who wants to work with you.

Zoe was a skinny psychiatrist who lived near me and we met at Follow Coffee in Ballymena, an expansive coffee shop with the best coffee and cheese toasties that made you moan. She was tall, obsessed with long-distance running and ate clean. That's three things we didn't have in common. "I've followed you on LinkedIn for years." I had 18,000 followers at this stage and hadn't spoken to most of them.

"A psychiatrist on a business platform; tell me more?" I asked.

"My clients are stressed out businesspeople. The way you write speaks to my heart. I've actually wanted this moment for a long time." She giggled, coy. Clearly she's not normally this forward and I liked it. Why do men always have to make the first move? It's cool when women take control. "Can you sign your book for me?" she purred.

"Happy to. Where's the copy?"

"In my car," said Zoe.

My phone rang, "I have to take this call. Give me a few minutes."

"I'll take care of the bill and get the book," said Zoe.

I like her style. No nonsense and does what she wants.

You can tell a lot about someone by how they treat other people. Zoe was criticising the staff about slow service and not refilling her cup. I didn't like her tone or her condescending manner. I cleared my throat. She wasn't expecting me to be finished from my call so quickly. I was cold-called by someone about my mobile tariff and politely declined.

Zoe flashed a smile. Too late, I had seen everything. "Good luck in the future, you're going to need it," I said to her.

"You've just turned down the best sex you're ever going to have," threatened Zoe.

"I've already had the best sex I've ever had and it was with myself!"

Not the answer I wanted to give, but I didn't have enough time to work on a witty retort.

After the Zoe disappointment, I met up with Orla near her home at Yoko. It had a reputation as one of the best Asian fusion restaurants in Northern Ireland, so I couldn't wait to try it.

The weather took a turn and storm warnings advised everyone not to drive unless it was urgent.

This was a second date, so I considered it a big step forward. Orla called me. "It's too dangerous for you to come to Coleraine tonight in this weather. Let's meet halfway."

"So we're both in danger?" I asked.

"I don't want anything happening to you, Niraj. Let's meet in Ballymena. Please drive safe."

How thoughtful and considerate was that? She was worried about me safely driving sixty minutes in a storm and was prepared to come and meet me halfway. This was one of the nicest things anyone had ever done for me.

I choose Galgorm Kitchen, one of the many delicious restaurants owned by the Galgorm Manor, a luxurious hotel in Ballymena.

Orla was vegetarian and I wanted her to have the best options. I grew up with a vegetarian family, married a veggie and my daughter is one too. So I always go the extra mile to make sure they have a good evening when eating out.

When Orla arrived, the wind was howling and the rain hit you hard in all directions. I rushed out with my umbrella and it immediately went U-shaped from the intense weather. "I need to win the lottery and move to Mallorca," shouted Orla over the howling wind.

As we dried off inside, Orla asked about my dating history. I was more interested in her dating history. Asking questions and really understanding is one of the most important skills in business. As a social worker with no side hustle or business interests, it was cool how she embraced this without even knowing it.

"What are the men like on Match?" I asked. Although you shouldn't copy the competition, you need to be aware of them and what their strengths and weaknesses are.

Orla took out her mobile and showed me. Men with terrible selfies. Shadows. Bad lighting, awkward poses. Quite a few resembled serial killers.

"That's not the worst part," said Orla. She showed the messages they had sent. Every single guy hit on her straight away with comments like, "Y'alright?", "Fancy meeting up?", "You're too fit to be single" or "I want to eat you up". Yes, another human being actually uttered those words!

I once read a great business quote by Jeffrey Gitomer, "It's not what you say, it's how someone perceives what you say." Be careful with the words you use. Don't just throw words out there. Also, you don't jump in too quickly and ask someone to marry you on the first date, not unless you're Indian.

We enjoyed a delicious dinner. I had a chickpea and sweetcorn burger and always try to avoid meat around vegetarians and vegans.

"Do you always treat women this well?"

"Why are you being so nice to me?" I didn't mean to blurt it out. With my terrible dating experiences, I had every right to ask.

"Kindness is a superpower," Orla replied innocently.

"Stop quoting me."

"Great minds think alike."

"You're quoting me again," I replied louder.

Orla calmed me down by taking my hand. "Not everything is a competition. I don't care if you're rich or popular. Just be kind and loving."

"I can do that with you."

"No. You have to do it with everyone, otherwise you're wasting my time, Niraj."

Wow. That statement knocked me down a peg and Orla was right. It made perfect sense.

"Let's get out of here," she suggested.

"Are we going back to your place?" I asked hopefully.

"My daughter is at home."

"Wonderful. How is she getting on at school?" That's what I should have said. Instead I asked, "Can you throw her out somewhere?"

Judging by Orla's shocked reaction, I shouldn't have said that. "She's a teenager and she drives me mad, but no … all good comes to those who wait."

Lightening cracked the sky and the wind shook her beat-up Ford Fiesta.

I escorted Orla to her car with my umbrella. "Where to next?" I asked.

The wind blew my umbrella away. "How about we go umbrella shopping?" she suggested. "There are shops near my house."

"Name the time and place," I asked.

"Saturday afternoon, Coleraine town centre. Then I'll make you something nice for dinner?"

I'd not had a third date for … I don't even think I'd had one since my divorce. I was more nervous for that, than anything else. Butterflies were having a party in my stomach.

When people are nervous they often can't eat or sleep. The former never affects me, I can eat regardless of mood. The sleepless nights took their toll. It was more excitement than fear, although the fear was there. What if it didn't work out? What if I had to start again? What do you even say on a third date?"

We met at Ground Espresso, where I had one of the best soya flat whites ever. The rain had stopped although it was a bitterly cold December with the wind howling. Christmas lights were up, yet not many people were shopping.

Orla told me her story, the ordeals she had to overcome in life, bringing up two children alone. I can't imagine how tough that must have been. She never had anger or regret in her voice. There was a calmness in her that made me feel safe.

"How did your daughters turn out?"

"They're not on drugs and didn't get pregnant. Mission accomplished."

She held out her hands to high-five me. We touched palms and our hands didn't move. Our eyes were fixated on each other. Her fingers slowly interlocked with mine.

"There's something I want to say ..." said Orla nervously.

"I won't break your heart," I assured her.

"I was going to ask if you had protection, but let's go with that," she smirked.

We left the coffee shop. My body shivered from the cold. I took off my scarf and jacket and gave them to Orla.

"What a gentleman."

"That was a stupid idea," I replied and jokingly took my jacket and scarf back. She grabbed my scarf and put it around her and we fought playfully.

"Winter is Coming," I cried out.

"You like *Game of Thrones*?" she asked with excitement.

"Best TV show ever."

"Have you been on the *Game of Thrones* tour?"

"Never."

"Niraj! Get ready for a third date that is going to blow your mind."

Instead of rushing back to Orla's, she took me to Portstewart beach, scene of the famous duel between Jaime and Bronn. We walk hand in hand on the freezing cold beach, sharing touching stories of our grandparents, who we miss dearly. In Indian tradition, it's custom to take care of your loved ones and never put them in a retirement home. I got to know my grandparents well when they lived with us during their final years. I think about them every day.

Next was Ballintoy Harbour, immortalised by Theon Greyjoy. The roads were narrow and almost impossible to drive along. That made the experience fun as cars would drive by so closely, wing mirrors would make contact. The irony of going to a medieval setting in a modern-day car didn't escape us. We discussed scary moments in our lives and our biggest fears. With Orla, she was scared that she had accepted that maybe she would never meet anyone. I was optimistic I would find someone, even though the back of my mind was playing different games. This loneliness brought us close together.

Finally, we had a warm, soothing hot-chocolate drink and made our way to the Dark Hedges where the trees on either side of the road romantically meet in the middle. It was where Arya Stark escaped King's Landing and the scenery was utterly beautiful.

The Dark Hedges was in the middle of nowhere. It was so

cold, the tourists didn't even turn up. The wind howled. We took selfies and looked at all the selfies we had taken.

"We look good together," said Orla.

She was right. I felt calm around her. The worries of the world, the economy and everything else faded away when she was with me.

You always want the perfect moment. At the top of the Eiffel Tower with glamorous views of Paris. Walking hand in hand on a glorious beach in the Caribbean with soothing water for miles around. In the green English countryside with a Fortnum & Mason-style picnic with well-behaved children who listen to your every word and respect you.

Sometimes the best moments are spontaneous.

"How was that for the third date?" she asked.

My eyes softened. I cupped Orla's face and didn't say a word.

"I was speechless after the *Game of Thrones* tour as well," said Orla.

"It's not that."

"Then what is it?"

"I've just met the woman I want to spend the rest of my life with," I said.

I kissed her with all the love in my heart. She pulled me close and it was absolute heaven.

A week later, I spent Christmas with Orla's family. You can never take a client for granted in business, same goes for dating. You have to keep paying attention and keep doing more to make the other person happy; otherwise, they lose process and go elsewhere.

Christmas was surrounded by Orla's four cats and her loud, loving, opinionated Catholic family.

Luckily, her family had researched me and realised I was a good person, or at least not a psychopath.

I've always been a dog person. Walking with them, petting them, playing with them, is such a joy. Cats were a new experience. They don't wag their tail and jump with joy when you arrive home. When you sit comfortably on the sofa and get up to make a cup of tea they steal your space, then give you a dirty look to say "don't even think about it".

Two weeks later, Orla met my family. She was vegetarian, worked for the NHS and respected her elders, so she was practically Indian. They adored her and I was welcomed into our house as one of our own.

A few days later, I announced on LinkedIn that I had met someone. That after all my pain, suffering, loneliness, setbacks, bad luck and disappointments, I had found true love. The post went viral. It reached almost 1,000,000 views with thousands of private messages of congratulations and support.

I felt like I had accomplished something truly amazing. It wasn't an award or a big commission cheque or a pay rise. It was something way more important.

Twelve months later, Orla and I moved in together, celebrated our first anniversary and are living happily ever after.

Business Lesson Learned

To succeed in business, you need to understand process.

Sales is a skill that needs to be learned, yet most people don't learn it. People can drop out at any stage for a variety of reasons: budget, lack of interest or they find somebody else.

Not everyone you meet is a potential client, just like not everyone you meet on the dating circuit is a match. It's okay to say no and move on. Being honest is key, although doing it with tact and humanity is more important.

Share testimonials. They matter and people buy into social proof.

The parallel between sales and dating is incredible. The main difference is that you only have to win once in dating. In sales and business, you have to understand sales process and keep working that funnel to win new business.

Once you win a client, don't stop and move into someone else. Keep nurturing that relationship. Keep adding value. Never take it for granted and always communicate clearly.

AFTERTHOUGHT

People aren't bad at selling, they're badly trained. Business owners need to stop thinking they're too good to do sales. Marketing needs to understand sales and sales needs to understand marketing. Boards of directors need to stop thinking of sales and LinkedIn coaching as a cost. It's NEVER a cost, only an investment.

One of the bests ways to grow your business is to tell your personal story. It's how people connect with you on a deeper level and see past your job title.

If you got value from reading *Business Growth: Lessons Learned from Dating, Divorce and Falling in Love*, then I'd be grateful if you could take a selfie, post it on social media and tag me in.

LinkedIn: https://uk.linkedin.com/in/nkapur
Twitter: Nirajwriter
Instagram: nirajkapur

GETTING RESULTS FOR YOUR BUSINESS

To get better results for yourself, your business or your team, message me on LinkedIn or email:
niraj@everybodyworksinsales.com

SEE WHAT OTHERS HAVE SAID ABOUT MY SPEAKING

Niraj did a cracking job. He was engaging, charismatic, funny and the delegates loved him. 45 minutes on stage with no PowerPoint or notes.

Jonny Fulton, MD, Foxwylie Event Management.

Niraj gave the best speech of the summit and is amazing when you think about how many top speakers were there. You made us laugh, you made us cry. Well done.

Steven Dryden-Hall, founder, Boom Seven

I've had so many delegates tell me how much they loved Niraj's speech and how much they learned about sales. You put so much effort into giving a speech with no props, notes or PowerPoint.

Amy Romaine, marketing manager, The Ready Group

It was a great talk. I learned so much about sales and you spoke in such an engaging way. You were funny, moving and everyone was talking about how you gave loads of value as well.

Oliver Waters, co-founder and CEO, Orbit

A fantastic and engaging speaker, one of the best I have seen.

Richard Ashton, director, Ardeema Solutions

You engaged with the audience and took them on a journey with you and what an incredible journey. Well done.

Suzy Beech, global director of sales, Toppan Digital Language

Niraj was a fabulous speaker, just unbelievable.

Sonya Perkins, regional sales manager, Aztec Commercial Cleaning

SEE WHAT OTHERS HAVE SAID ABOUT MY COACHING AND TRAINING

Niraj made a positive impact. He's an excellent communicator of ideas and his sessions are very practical with a strong actionable follow-up plan. I would not hesitate to recommend him.

Tom Turnbull, commercial director, Lyonsdown.

Niraj was recommended by a colleague. He helped me change my mindset, gave me more confidence and the tools to use LinkedIn. He keeps you accountable for your actions and cares about you achieving your goals.

Gillian Etherington, founder, Human Touch HR Solutions

Working with Niraj has been the best thing I could have done. Not only does he help you with your sales technique, he also coaches you on a personal basis.

Annie Thompson, owner, Cornerstone FD

Since working with Niraj, I'm more engaging in demos, better at handling objections, and have become more self-aware and confident and closed more deals as a result.

Ehsan Ali, account executive, Ultimate AI

I would 100% recommend Niraj as a sales trainer and a speaker. I have worked with him across two different companies. He's warm, engaging and feedback from the attendees was incredible.

Emma Kennedy, marketing manager, ATG Group

I was recommended Niraj by a colleague and he facilitated a session for Enterprising Women Network on softer skills to drive more sales. Feedback from attendees was fantastic. Niraj overdelivered, was interactive, energetic, fun and likeable.

Kelli McRoberts, manager, Carrick Enterprise.

Niraj is an incredible coach and mentor, his endless supply of experience and knowledge is game-changing for any sales team. He coaches my sales team on LinkedIn, and helped us establish sustainable habits to ensure long-term growth and success.

Vince Cain, social impact project manager, 20/Twenty

Niraj is nothing but brilliant. Simple practical advice that's easy to implement with great results.

Sam Furr, founder, Tappable.

90 more recommendations can be found on my LinkedIn profile.
https://uk.linkedin.com/in/nkapur
Feel free to follow me there for more valuable business, sales and LinkedIn content.

BOOK RECOMMENDATIONS

LinkedIn

Content DNA by John Espirian, smart and insightful, much like John.
The Ultimate LinkedIn Sales Guide by Daniel Disney, a vital easy-to-use guide.
The Million Pound LinkedIn Message by Daniel Disney, another excellent book.

Sales

The B2B Sales Top Tips Guidebook by Jim Irving. All of Jim's books are worth reading, this one is my favourite.
Six-Figure Sales Secrets by Marcus Chan. Build your pipeline and close deals fast.
Heart-Powered Sales by Robin Treasure. A modern book on selling.

Kids' books also relevant to business

I Want to Be in Sales When I Grow Up by John Barrows, simple and effective
Billy the Goat and the Five Pound Note by Robin Waller, my nephew loved this.
Ralphy's Rules for Living the Good Life by Talar Herculian Coursey, a book on kindness from a wonderful author who I'm lucky to call a friend.

Business

Compound Effect by Darren Hardy, on getting better one per cent every day.
Legacy by James Kerr, lessons learned from the All Blacks rugby team.
Your Next Five Moves by Patrick Bet-David, an immigrant who found his fortune through excellence.

Habits

High Performance Habits by Brendon Burchard, one of the world's top personal development coaches shares his advice.
Atomic Habits by James Clear. I read this before it became a worldwide best-seller. Vital reading.
Tools of Titans by Tim Ferris, what are the routines, reading habits of the top people?

Marketing

Hook Point by Brendan Kane, some brilliant ideas in here.
1-Page Marketing Plan by Allan Dib. Helped me see marketing in a new way.
Known by Mark Schaefer. A mixture of personal branding and marketing.

Biographies

The Shoe Maker by Joe Foster. From the co-founder of Reebok.
Leading by Alex Ferguson. From the world's most successful football manager.
The Essential Wooden by John Wooden, a legend in his field.

Others

Energize by Simon Alexander Ong, a mix of personal development, business and creating more energy.
JOLT! by Larry Long Jr. The last chapter about Larry's late father is worth the entire book.
Awesomely Simple by John Spencer. A great leader in business.
Everybody Works in Sales and *The Easy Guide to Sales* by Niraj Kapur are both available on Amazon.
How to Sell When Times Are Tough by Niraj Kapur is a 52-page ebook available on Bookboon.

THANK YOUS

Daniel Disney and Steve Burton for your real friendship and advice.

Loren Greiff, Michael Hanson, Susie Mathieson, Katie Thomas and Talar Herculian Coursey for always recommending me for work.

Natalie Costa, Larry Long Jr, Corina Goetz, Elly Yule, Kieren O'Connor, Aisha Saddiq, Charlotte Moyle, Marcus Chan, Susan Fang, Simon Alexander Ong, Laurie Wang, Sally Maeir-Yip, Darryl Praill, John Spence, Amanda Rowe, Lois Cliff, Timea Kadar, Sinead Glennon, Chris Postill, Debbie Lewis and Reely Rajan for your kindness and support.

Laura Tejada and Louise Ansell for lifting me up and always being so positive.

John Espirian for his coaching and love of pineapple on pizza.

Clare Carroll for the cover design.

Lisa De Caux for editing, Catherine Williams for typesetting, and Karen Morton for proofreading.

To my virtual assistant of 3 years, Nicola Case, you're a rock star.

Brilliant co-founders of the Northern Ireland Sales Summit: Jim Irving and Colly Graham.

My accountability partner, the excellent motivational speaker, Chris Moon.

To my new friends in Northern Ireland: Scott Bingham and Olivia, Claire and Lisa, Domilia Timonyte, Emma Kennedy.

To Freya for inspiring me every day and to my ex-wife, Priyanka, I'm delighted you found happiness in the new chapter of your life.

To Rachel, for making it all happen.

ABOUT THE AUTHOR

After twenty-three years in London running sales teams from *The Guardian* newspaper group to FTSE 100 businesses, Niraj wanted to raise the standards of sales, so he wrote *Everybody Works in Sales* which was in the Amazon Top 100 on twenty-nine occasions.

He then set up his own sales coaching and training company to keep businesses accountable to help them achieve results. He's delivered LinkedIn Training and Sales Coaching to over 400 solopreneurs and SMEs including staff at Barclays, NatWest, Sainsbury's and Google.

Skills people have benefitted from are prospecting, role-plays, mentoring, LinkedIn training, LinkedIn content writing, profile optimisation, overcoming objections, email writing, sales language, listening skills and presentation skills.

In 2021 and 2022, Niraj was announced as a Top Sales Influencer in the World to Follow by Salesforce.

In November 2021, he was announced as a Top 10 Linkedin Voice in Sales by LinkedIn.

In his free time, Niraj plays drums in a rock band, raises

money for charities like Movember and serves as an ambassador for Milton Keynes Hospital Cancer Unit.

INDEX